LITERARY ICONS OF NEPAL
(Part 1)

Gopal Parajuli

Translator
Chandra Gurung

Editor
Mahesh Paudyal

Ratna Pustak Bhandar
Kathmandu, Nepal

D1490306

Literary Icons of Nepal
(Part 1)
Gopal Parajuli

Publisher : Ratna Pustak Bhandar, Kathmandu, Nepal

Translator : Chandra Gurung

Editor : Mahesh Paudyal

Edition : First, 2015

© : Author

Printed in Nepal

ISBN: 978-9937-33-072-2

Literary Icons of Nepal: Intellectual Heritage at a Glimpse

I am delighted to have this opportunity to go through *Lirerary Icons of Nepal* (Part 1) by Gopal Parajuli. This book records the biographies of prominent literary writers, thinkers, critics, historians, linguists and educationists, starting from Vidyapati, the renowned poet of Maithili literature (b, 1350 AD). This is indeed a significant work aiming at the preservation of the history of Nepali literary heritage. The compiler, translator and the editor deserve accolades for introducing the gems of Nepal and maintaining the recorded history for the posterity.

This book comprises of fifty pioneers' biographies with pertinent details of life, living and the contributions they made for the making of Nepali society, culture and literature. The details give a glimpse of the learned creators' scholarly pursuits amid the ground realities they faced and provide readers moments to be proud of them. The book provides an inventory to learn about Nepal's important creative minds and their works, and paves a way for Nepal's literary and cultural identity.

Every society's identity depends upon the art of thinking, learning and writing. Human societies are known for their rich intellectual tradition and culture. A society without literary expressions has hardly anything to offer to the world civilization. It is not easy to think what would happen to the Hindu culture and tradition without the *Vedas* and epics like the *Ramayana* and the *Mahabharata*, and to the Western civilization in the absence of Greek and Roman literary and philosophical writings. The world would be a void with no direction, and human beings in the world would be like passengers in a ship who notice no lighthouse that signals the approach of a harbor to anchor their ship. From this perspective, thinkers, writers, critics, linguists and historians are the pathfinders of a society. It is in their works from which the society assumes its immortality. William Shakespeare aptly says that 'powerful rhyme' is the living record of memory that remains unaffected by 'death', the 'ending doom' and the 'sluttish time' 'to find room even in the eyes of all posterity.' This book, to my mind, ventures to let not only children, but even the adults recollect their past glory, to rethink about and revere ones who have saved the Nepali civilization and culture.

June 26, 2014

Amma Raj Joshi, Ph.D.
Professor and Head
Central Department of English
Tribhuvan University

Editor's Acknowledgements

Ever since I lay my hand in the works of Gopal Prajuli a decade back, two things had been tickling my mind. First, if his works were translated into English, they would present the entire intellectual tradition of Nepal in front of English-educated children of our times. Second, such works, if launched in English, would make the task of researchers—both local and foreign—easy in a number of ways. Of and on, I myself started the task, but the idea never moved to any accomplishment. Finally, I asked one of my brightest students and a creative writer Chandra Gurung to take up the task, and like an obedient student, he happily took up the assignment. Within a year or so, he furnished the first draft, upon which, I was expected to act. It was more of a blessing for me, because, through my student, my own dream was coming true. And here is the book, finally, a work I voluntarily took up as a mark of my respect for the senior writer Parajuli.

For the translation work, the translator and I agreed upon a policy. Books named in Nepali are not translated for the simple reason that proper nouns are not translated. Second, owing to the fact they have appeared in unmanageably numerous locations, we decided to leave the dates in Bikram Sambat (BS) as they are instead of translating them into Anno Domini (AD). A date in AD can be achieved by subtracting 57 from the date in BS, though sometimes, the dates do not accurately coincide.

I thank the author Gopal Parajuli for allowing me this rare opportunity. I am thankful to Chandra Gurung, whose contribution will be rated exceptionally high in the days to come, when English education shall further tighten its grip across the world.

Suggestions to improve the book shall always be welcomed.

Mahesh Paudyal

A Few Words from the Author

In my schooldays, I was highly conscious and interested to know about the lives of our native literary creators. As I grew up, I thought that like myself, other school-going children would also be curious and interested to know about the lives of such great literary personalities.

So I thought, if I introduced such ever-memorable creators to the children of the upcoming generation, they would certainly increase and enrich their knowledge. Furthermore, such personalities might, in turn, directly or indirectly encourage and inspire the new generation to follow their meritorious footsteps.

Thus, I started writing about such creators by collecting their biographical information and facts, and their works i.e. the literary legacy they had left behind at our disposal.

In the initial period, I doubted whether I could really accomplish this task. I also didn't know how the native readers would take my initiative. But as I continued writing, I found myself encouraged by my loving readers.

My well-wishers and amicable friends as well as my esteemed readers, time and often, advised and suggested me to present the original versions of the works in English language, so that even the non-native readers will know about our literary icons, who have enriched our literature and culture. And that resulted into the production of this book.

I hope, this translated version will be quite useful and beneficial to foreign but friendly readers, as was the Nepali version to my Nepali readers. I hope, they would definitely enjoy reading about our unforgettable writers and philosophers.

Finally, I would like to express my sincere thanks to my benevolent friend Chandra Gurung who translated these essays with an enthusiastic spirit, to Mahesh Paudyal, who edited this compilation and to Toya Nath Bhattarai who carefully read the draft from cover to cover and suggested ways to make it reader-friendly. I express my sincere thanks to Prof. Dr. Ammaraj Joshi, head, Central Department of English, Tribhuvan University for writing an intellectual foreword to my book in spite of his busy schedule. I am equally thankful to my publishers, Ratna Pustak Bhandar, and my well-wishers and friends for their untiring inspiration.

September, 2014   **Gopal Parajuli**

CONTENTS

Vidyapati:
The Great Maithili Poet

Vidyapati is a great poet of Maithili literature. Numerous people speak and write Maithili language as their mother tongue in Dhanusha, Mahottari, and Sarlahi districts of Nepal. Vidyapati is the best-known poet of Maithili literature both in Nepal and India. People, who speak Maithili, are many in both the countries. Vidyapati is not only an honorable poet, but also a respectable author for the lovers of Nepal's literature.

Nobody claims the exact year when Vidyapati was born, but intellectuals estimate that he was born around 1407 BS.

There was a province named Mithila in the Tarai region of Nepal. Inhabitants of the region were called 'Maithil' and the language they spoke was called 'Maithili'. There was a village named Biski in Mithila state. That village lies in Madhuwani District of India at present. Vidayapati was born in the same village.

Vidyapati's father was called Ganapati Thakur and mother Ganga Devi. Vidyapati learned how to read and write from his father at home. He knew many things within a short period of time because he was keenly interested in learning. Later, he got education from Hari Mishra, an erudite man of Mithila.

Mithila has a rich tradition of scholarship, represented by learned scholars and philosophers. The King of Mithila respected Vidhapati's father as a reputed priest, and so, the latter would frequently visit the royal palace. Vidyapati used to go to the palace with his father since childhood. He would talk about knowledge and wisdom since his early age. He often engaged in study. So, he was very wise and intelligent.

Since he read a lot of Sanskrit scriptures at a young age, he knew many things about religion. The King of Mithila and his people were impressed at the knowledge and sharp mind of Vidyapati. That's why, he was highly honored and appreciated in Mithila.

Vidyapati had started writing poems as a child. He wrote about medicine, and also wrote descriptions of different places and religious subjects. He has written many books of different genres like songs, hymns, poems, short epics, long epics, plays, stories, description of expedition and hunting, warfare, memoirs, astrology, Ayurveda and nature cure, domestic medicinal science, proverbs etc. Such a wide range of scholarship made him an erudite poet at an early age of twenty.

Vidyapati was proficient in Sanskrit, Maithili and Abahattha, a vernacular language. He has written books in all these three languages. Even now, we cannot ascertain the number of books he wrote. Following books have been published, though.

In Sanskrit his works were: 1. Bhu-Parikrama, 2. Purush-Pariksha (Part 1-7), 3. Shaiva Sarvashwasaar Pramaanbhoot, 4. Likhanawali, 5. Ganga Wakyayawali, 6. Bibhagsar, 7. Danwakyawali, 8. Gaya Pattalak, 9. Durga Bhakti Tarangini, 10. Manimanjari , 11. Varsha, 12. Braatya, 13. Byadhi Bhakti Tarangini.

In Abahathata he had written: 1. Kritilata (Part 1-2), 2. Kriti Pataka (Part 1-2).

In Maithili he wrote: 1. Gorakchhabijaya Natak, 2. Maithili Padawali.

Vidyapati has also written many other books, which have not been published yet. Manuscripts of some of these books have been kept safely in Nepal National Library and National Archives. The manuscripts of the books kept there include: 1. Kirtilata (part 3 and 4), 2. Kirtipataka (part 3 and 4), 3. Padawali (Tarauni Padawali, Ram Bhadrapur Padawali, Vaishnav Padawali, Nepali Padawali, and many more, that amount to approximately three thousand verse forms) 4. Likhanawali 5. Danawakyawali (part 2 and 3) 6. Vaidyarahasyam, 7. Madhawanal Katha 8. Vidyapati Geet (part 1 and 2), 9. Durga Bhakti Tarangini (part 2).

Some manuscripts of Vidyapati's books have also been found in Calcutta, Darvangah, Patna and Madhuwani areas of India and it is conjectured that his books might be in other parts of the world, too. Still his works are being looked for. Thus, there are many works of him.

Like his birth that has no factual evidence, no one has asserted for sure when Vidyapati died. It is assumed that he died around 1496 B. S. At that time, he was 89 years old. He has written in one of his poems that he would die on the third day of the bright half of the lunar month of Kartik. On that basis, it is supposed that he died in the month of Kartik. He, thus, is also recognized as a prophet.

Vidyapati is known as 'Mahakavi'—a great poet—in Maithili literature, and is accorded high honor and respect in both countries, Nepal and India. After hundred years of his death, a book named *Vidyapati Padawali* was published. It was translated into Nepali by Dhirendra Premarshi, and the Royal Nepal Academy has published it.

Even though Vidyapati is no more, he will be alive in his verses forever. His birth anniversary is celebrated every year in both Nepal and India. In his commemoration, different programs and functions are organized in both the countries. Much research has been done on him and many books and magazines are published, too. Many people have received great titles for their scholarship on the life and works of Vidyapati. Nepal Government, Postal Service Department has issued a postal stamp with his photo as a mark of homage to him. He is among the greatest artists we have ever had in the literary firmament of Nepal.

■

First Great Poet Udayananda Aryal

Nwaran garai banaka kuna singha banchhan
Singhai sakal chha tinaka tarbarpan chhan.

[Lion, the king of the forest, is not defined by a name he is given at his birth. He has his own power and his own weapons from birth.]

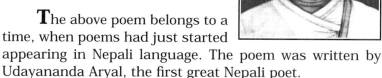

The above poem belongs to a time, when poems had just started appearing in Nepali language. The poem was written by Udayananda Aryal, the first great Nepali poet.

A poet who writes about a person and does a daring work for the nation is called a heroic poet. A poet who writes amusing poems is called a 'rasik' or romantic poet. Udayananda Aryal is both a heroic and a romantic poet. There is a great contribution of him in Nepali literature. He is a great poet of the earliest phase of Nepali poetry. Among the epics he wrote, *Prithivindrodaya* is by far the most famous one.

It is believed that Udayananda Aryal was born in 1812 BS though the date has not been confirmed by any research. His father's name was Bishweshower Aryal but his mother's name has not been ascertained so far. No one knows where he was born. People assume that he was born in Gorkha. Some other people opine that he was born either in Kathmandu or in Saptari District. There are some scholars who think that he was the nephew of Saktiballav Aryal, a celebrated playwright and poet. Whatever has been derived about him is from his books and from chronicles of Aryal genealogy.

Udayananda Aryal was the only son of his father. He did not get the opportunity to attend any school, because there were no schools at that time. He learned to read from his father at home. He had a sound environment to read at home because his father was a famed astrologer and scholar. After he became adult, Udayananda held a government job. It was the then Prime Minister Bhimsen Thapa who gave him the job. He became a clerk and arbitrator in the gorvernment. It is not known at which place and position he held the job, nor does anyone know the time period of his tenure. Aryal clan history shows, he had seventeen children.

Udayananda was a social worker too. He constructed a temple, an inn and a pond for general public's use. In Laxmi Narayan Temple he built at Bairawa of Saptari District in 1893 BS, it is found that he had offered a bell. He also constructed the Temple of Kankalini Devi at Bhardaha of Saptari.

Udayananda was an astrologer too. He believed that if we drink the water we bathe in and the water offered to God in a puja, leprosy would be cured. He himself cured the leprosy of many people. It is known that he had a good knowledge of Ayurveda. He also had sound knowledge of many languages. He wrote poems in all languages he knew since childhood. He was a multi-talented poet. He has written poems in seven languages: Nepali, Sanskrit, Urdu, Persian, Hindi, Maithili, and Newari. While reading today, it is rather difficult for us to comprehend the language of his days. Still, we can easily surmise that it was not an ordindary thing for a man to write poems in seven languages.

Udayananda once wrote a poem about his father in contemporary Nepali language. A stanza of that poem goes like this:

*Shri Bishweshwar naam chaudisa bise pura ta
    jyotismaha
Marjile ta Kirata rajya ti gaya Hindupatiko jaha
Jukti buddhi lagai ambal bhayo yasta aru chhan
    kaha*

Rajalai rijhai Kausiki nikat birta Madeshma bhayo
Un dindekhi Madeshama ta sabako bas Bairawama
bhayo

[Bishweshwar had earned a lot of fame as an acclaimed astrologer everywhere. He went to the Kirat's land, which was at the time under a Hindu king. He used his trick and wit and became successful. No one was like him. Pleasing the king, he got land in Kaushik in Madhes. From that day, all his people started living in Bairawa, a place in Madhes.]

Following are his published epics:

In Nepali: 1. Purano Batko Arji, 2. Prithivindrodaya, 3. Betal Pachchisi, 4. Bamsha Brittanta.

In Sanskrit: 1. Someshwar Vijaya Varnan, 2. Kulvarnan, 3. Duswapna Dukhahar Strota.

Apart from these works, he had written *Ramayan*, a long epic, and *Veersikka* and *Daskumarcharitra* two short epics. But these epics have not been published till now. His collection of poems too is yet to be published.

Regarding Udayananda, historians of Nepali literature have talked a lot in their books. Many writers opine that he is the Aadimahakavi, the first great poet of Nepal. A book named *Pundit Udayananda Aryal: Jeevani ra Kriti* (Udayananda Aryal: Life and Works) has been prepared.

Researchers opine that Udayananda died in 1894 BS. A long time after his death in 2047 BS, his descendents institutionalized a literary association named 'Udayananda Memorial Trust' in his name. The Trust distributes awards to writers, historians and linguists every year.

It is also found that critics of Nepal and India have honored him with the title 'Aadimahakavi'—the first great poet—because his contribution in the first phase of Nepali poetry has not only been commendable, but also a trend-setter. His contribution in the field of Nepali epics will be cherished for ever.

Hermit Khaptad Baba

Khaptad Baba is supposed to be one of the most long-lived hermits of this era. He had an unprecedented store of knowledge and an extraordinary conscience. Generally, it is said that a wise super-human like him gets born in a hundred years of time in the world. His works of art are the proofs of his knowledge and conscience. It is assumed that his  followers and well-wishers in Nepal, India, Sri Lanka and Bhutan, are in terms of billions.

Khaptad Baba was born in Jammu, a city in Kashmir province of India. No one knows when he was born. But it is assumed that he was born around 1866 BS. Swami Dr. Prapannacharya researched about him and concluded that Khaptad Baba died after a long life of one hundred and eighty-seven years. So, his year of birth is assumed to be 1866 BS.

Khaptad Baba's father's name was Janak Sharma Dogra and his mother's name Gauri. His name at home was Shivanath Dogra. He took his basic education at home. But he completed his further studies from Britain.

Khaptad Baba acquired the degree of MBBS from Britain. After he returned from Britain to India, he himself established a hospital in Jammu-Kashmir and started working there. He served the sick people without any fee.

One day, a strange incident occured. Khaptad Baba was treating a sick lad. In the course of this treatment, the child died. Declaring that the child was dead, he gave the dead body to his mother. In extreme grief, the mother kept her dead son on her lap and sat crying in the garden outside the hospital.

The mother was extremely poor. She did not have other offspring. Her husband had also died long back. She had lived in a rented room because she was treated badly by her father-in-law and mother-in-law. For survival, she had to depend upon wage-labor. The infant son was the only hope for her future support. Since her son was no more, her patience crossed its limit, and she cried all day and finally fell unconscious.

Coincidently, a hermit hailing from somewhere, happened to pass by. Khaptad Baba, in his physician's uniform, was trying to calm and console the woman. As soon as the woman saw the hermit, she fell onto his legs and cried even more pathetically. The hermit's heart was filled with compassion. Chanting some mantras, he sprinkled some holy water from his *kamandalu*—a water grail carried by ascetics—upon the dead body of the child.

Surprisingly, the child came back to consciousness, and started talking to his mother. Seeing the miracle, Khaptad Baba immediately put away his uniform, and kneeling down on the feet of the hermit, said, "O, the pious one! Please make me your disciple. All my pride has been defeated today. You revived a dead child whom I'd declared dead medically. At times, meditation and mantras happened to be greater than science. What use is my learned mind! I become your disciple right from this moment. Please impart me your knowledge."

The yogi accepted his plea. And then Khaptad Baba entered the order of the hermits. The yogi took him to many different places and taught him many thing. After some years, Khaptad Baba became Swami Sachidananda Saraswati. By that time, he had become a renowned scholar of these subjects: geography, history, religion, philosophy, natural medicine, meditation, culture etc.

Khaptad Baba came to Nepal thinking that the atmosphere of Nepal was most suitable for meditation. He visited many different places of Nepal. Ultimately, he chose Khaptad-Lek, a highland slope in the mountains of Doti District. He meditated there.

Slowly, his fame spread across the country. People started calling him 'Khaptad Baba' because of his stay in Khaptad. He had become a divine personage through the meditation he performed there. No any wild animals and beasts harmed him. He would rather caress tigers, lions and cheetahs without any daunt right before the people who came to see him. These wild beasts and predators never attacked the people sitting beside him. People would look at the sight with amazement.

Khaptad Baba wrote some books during his stay in Khaptad. He spent approximately fifty-five years there in high altitude. Clad only in a *dhoti* and a *khasto*—a wrap of homespun cloth—even in cold season, he would be engaged in deep meditation, and writing. People from far and wide reached there to see him. People from foreign land would also reach there and put their inquisitions on many different subjects. He would answer all of them satisfactorily. Sometime, he would come to Kathmandu and meditate at Budhanilkantha, a holy shrine in Kathmandu. Devotees would assemble there, too. He would give blessings and spiritual teachings. He would often jot down the lessons he was supposed to deliver. Such writings were summed up to many beautiful books. These books were published later. The books he wrote are as follows:

1. Bichar Vigyan (Science of Thoughts), 2. Swasthya Vigyan (Health Science), 3. Dharma Vigyan (Science of Religion) (Part 1, 2, 3 and 4), 4. Dharma Vigyan Sarsamchhep (Science of Religion in a Nutshell), 5. Ma ra Mero Kartavya (Me and My Duty), 6. Naridharma tatha Purushdharma (Woman's Discipline and Man's Discipline), 7. Aatmagyan (Knowledge of Self).

Khaptad Baba died on 17 Baisakh 2053 BS. Such a great ascetic's death is not considered death, but *samadhi* or *brahmalin*—dissolution into Brahma, the creator. His age was one hundred and eighty-seven at the time of death. He had already predicted the date of his own death to his disciples, and his prediction came out right.

An organization has been established in his commemoration after his death. This organization and Mahendra Sanskrit University have been publishing his books. His books are being read widely even today. Nepal government has issued a postal stamp with his image. Many researches are being carried out about him even today.

In fact, Khaptad Baba is a profound treasure of Nepal. He was a living icon of Hindu religion, culture and spiritual insights. His death caused a heavy loss that all the Nepalese have to bear with heavy hearts.

■

First Nepali Poet Bhanubhakta Acharya

Bharjanma ghaanstira mann diyi
  dhan kamayo
Naam kyei rahos pachhi bhanera
  kuwa khanayo
Ghansi daridra gharako tara buddhi
  kasto
Ma Bhanubhakta dhani bhaikana
  aaja yasto!

[He gathered fodder all his life, and earned a little. With it, he got a well dug up, hoping it would give him some face. Though a poor man he was, how benevolent were his thoughts! Fie on me, Bhanubhakta; I did nothing, though quite well-off.]

There is an interesting event that describes how Bhanubhakta Acharya grew up to become a poet. One day, he was walking near a stream. He was completely exhausted, for, he had walked for a long time before reaching there. He sat on a stone under a tree and fell asleep under the cool shade of the tree.

After a while, a Ghansi—grass-cutter—arrived. Singing a folk tune, he started gathering fodder. Bhanubhakta woke up hearing the song. He wanted to talk with the man; so, he asked, "What do you do with this grass, brother?"

Ghansi replied, "I want to earn some money by selling it. I will spend some of it to bring up my sons and daughters. I will save some. I have already saved a little."

Bhanubhakta enquired again, "What do you intend to do with the saving?"

Ghansi answered, "With some of my saving, I have got a well dug up. Now, I have a desire to have a shade built for travelers. This work will make me immortal after my death.

What is there to receive after death? I will work very hard, and achieve this dream at any cost."

Bhanubhakta was deeply moved by Ghansi's words. Though he was poor, Ghansi worked for the welfare of others. That day onwards, Bhanubhakta decided to devote himself to the well-being of others.

Bhanubhakta wanted to become famous. He realized that he had not done anything for others, though he came from a well-off family. While he was in deep thoughts, a flash of poetry occurred to his mind. The verses in the beginning of this article are some lines from the same.

Bhanubhakta Acharya became the first great poet of Nepali language and literature. He is, therefore, known 'Aadikavi', the first poet. Though there had been poets before him, none had written in the language of the general people, and on one had gained so much of popularity as Bhanubhakta Acharya did.

Acharya was born on 29th Ashadh, 1871 BS in a village called Ramgha of Tanahu in mid-western Nepal. His grandfather Shrikrishna Acharya was well-versed in Sanskrit language. Bhanubhakta studied Sanskrit at an early age with him, but soon he developed a very keen interest in Nepali language, the language of the common people. He translated the *Ramayana* from Sanskrit into Nepali in his original style. He also composed many beautiful and elegant poems that have remained all-time favorites of many readers till today. In addition to the *Ramayana*, he also produced works such as *Prashnottar, Bhaktamala* and *Badhushiksha* that have become permanent treasures of Nepali literature for all times.

Bhanubhakta was an educated person; so he could write poems when he wanted. He understood that if he translated the holy *Ramayana* from Sanskrit into Nepali, he could help the uneducated people, who had no access to Sanskrit language. He produced the *Ramayana* in Nepali language, which is today famous as *Bhanubhaktako*

Ramayan. His translated *Ramayana* is a simple read, and extremely lucid in its flow. People, who are able to read only the Nepali alphabets, can also read the *Ramayana*. A few starting verses of his *Ramayana* read like this:

> *Ek din Narada Satyalok pugigaya lokko garaun hit bhani*
> *Brahma taahi thiya parya charanma khusi garaya pani.*

[One day, Sage Narad reached heaven with a desire to do *something* for the welfare of the world. Brahma, the creator, was there. Narad fell upon His feet and pleased Him.]

Bhanubhakta visited Kathmandu twice or thrice in his life. Once he stayed at Balaju before reaching Kathmandu. He composed a poem about this place. The two verses of this poem are given below:

> *Yati dinpachhi maile aaja Balaju dekhyan*
> *Prithivital bharima swarga ho jani lekhyan*

[After such a long time, I saw Balaju today and knew, it was paradise on earth.]

Bhanubhakta worked in a government office in Kathmandu. He was imprisoned at Kumarichowk because he had failed to keep the accounts. He did not remain quiet, even inside the prison. He translated much of the *Ramayana* there, and wrote a few scrap poems.

Bhanubhakta got entangled in a legal dispute about land with Giridhari Bhat. When the case was delayed, he wrote these verses addressed to a clerk at the court:

> *Kati ma garaun bhanchhan bholi-bholi*
> *Bholi-bholi bhani saba ghara bityo, baksiyos aaja jholi*

[How much should I do? You always postpone for the next day. Your postponement has jeopardized all my world now; take everything I have and finish me off.]

Bhanubhakta ridiculed the customs of his society through his poems.

Bhanubhakta had a strong desire to contribute immensely in his life. Social systems were not in his favor. He was neglected by time and contexts. He encountered many obstacles every day. He could not free himself from the trap of those hurdles. Whatever he did was marvelous, considering the highly conservative age he lived in.

Bhanubhakta passed away at the age of 54 in 1925 BS. His poems will always remind Nepali people of his contribution. As a poet, he has become a precious son of Mother Nepal. His half-size statue has been erected in front of Durbar High School to honor him. The earstwhile Durbar High School has now been named Bhanubhakta Memorial High School, after him.

There are several statues of Bhanubhakta in Nepal and abroad, especially in Darjeeling, Kalingpong, and Sikkim. He is a true poet of the entire Nepali nation. He has been declared a National Luminary.

■

Motiram Bhatta: A Star of Brief Living

Seldom can a country ignore someone who worked for the country even if he or she died prematurely. Such a citizen becomes immortal because of great and worthy deeds. Motiram Bhatta is one of such true sons of Mother Nepal, whom we remember as an immortal poet, though he died at an early age of 30.

Motiram Bhatta was born at Bhosiko Tole in Kathmandu in the month of Bhadra in 1923 BS. His father's name was Dayaram Bhatta and mother's name Ripumardini Devi.

Motiram Bhatta started living with his father in Kashi, a holy city in northern India, when he was merely five years old. His education began there. He studied Nepali, Urdu, and Persian languages until he was fifteen. Her returned to Kathmandu in 1937 BS and got married the same year.

As morning shows the day, Motiram was quite promising, right from his early age. He came to know about Bhanubhakta, the poet who had composed beautiful poems, on hearing the recitation of *Ramayana* at his own marriage ceremony. His interest to devote his time and labor to literature grew more after he heard folk songs sung by Daaureni, a woman involved in the collection of firewood, and Ghaseni, a woman grass-cutter. He developed profound love for his mother-tongue. With these inspirations, he published an original book of poetry called *Manodweg Prabah* in Banaras in the year 1938 BS.

Bhanubhakta was largely unknown to Nepali society, before the rise of Motiram Bhatta. Because of the efforts of

Motiram, Nepali society came to know about Bhanubhakta. Motiram Bhatta published "Baal Kanda" the first section of the Ramayana in 1941 BS, and the whole of the Ramayana in 1944 BS. Thus, he made it possible for Nepali people to enjoy the verses of the Ramayana.

Motiram Bhatta also wrote and published the biography of Bhanubhakta after conducting a research on the poet's life for three years. After this, hidden Bhanubhakta came to light. Since then, Motiram Bhatta has occupied a prominent place in Nepali language and literature.

Poet Motiram passed his high schools from Calcutta in 1948 BS. He appeared at the F.A. exam, equivalent to Proficiency Certificate Level, but was not successful. Collecting energy and enthusiasm to sit for the exam once again, he headed for Calcutta. He could not face the exam due to illness. However, by that time, he had acquired a deep knowledge of Sanskrit, Persian, Urdu, Hindi, Bengali and English languages, with his own efforts and hard labor.

There was such a rare intelligence in Motiram Bhatta. Consequently, he became the first Nepali journalist. Establishing a press in 1944 BS, he published the magazine Gorkha Bharat Jeevan. He came back to Kathmandu in the same year and opened a library in the name of Motikrishna Company to fulfill the needs of the public for knowledge.

Motiram wrote poems and encouraged his friends to do so. His main works include Manodweg Prabah, Gajendra Moksha, Prahlad Bhaktikatha, Shakuntala, Padmawati and Pikadoot. This way, Motiram enriched Nepali language and literature with his beautiful poetry and ghazals, besides his research works and critical writings.

Motiram always told the truth. He never concealed anything from people in order to deceive them. He had a deep attachment with Nepali language and literature. He never developed a desire to earn fame. He was always conscious of morality, duty and responsibility.

Not only did Motiram Bhatta work for Nepali language and literature in just one aspect, he also wrote the biography of the first poet Bhanubhakta Acharya. He strengthened Nepali literature with the publication of his anthology *Manodweg Prabah*. He raised awareness among poets to write poem, and helped them with techniques of versification. He attempted to enrich the store of Nepali language and literature with his many original and translated works. Besides, he wrote ghajals and poems of *Bhaktirasa* and *Hasyarasa*—containing devotional and humorous ethos—respectively.

Motiram lived a very short life of 30 years only from Kushe Aushi, the last day of the dark fortnight of the month of Bhadra, to the same day of Kushe Aushi thirty years later. Still, even in such a short span of living, he left incalculable credit to Nepali language and literature. He passed away on the day of Kushe Aushi in 1953 BS, but remained an immortal hero, because of his service to the nation.

He is honored as a poet *par excellence* and a hero of Nepali language and literature. For, who can forget a talent that gave us immortal lines like the following?

Achal jhanda pharkos pharaphara gari Kantipurima
Ripuko mann tharkos tharathara gari chhina gharima
Yavanle raj garda kati patita Hindusthala bhayo
Phagat Nepalko muluka bachi kanchan rahigayo.

[Let the firm flag flutter in Kantipur
Let the foes deter, trembling in terror
How low did India sink when the aliens ruled?
Nepal remained spared and was thus left pure.]

■

Siddhidas Amatya: A Great Newari Poet

Talk to your compatriots, wherever you meet them and show them all the respect you can. Wipe people's sorrow, as much as you can. Feed the hungry, clothe the naked and manage jobs for those out of work. These are the duties of a countryman.

This is a saying of Siddhidas Amatya. With more than fifty works in Nepali or Newari language to his credit, he is the author who made Newari language and literature quite rich. He is called 'Mahakavi'— the great poet—of modern Newari literature. With many works in Newari language, he has contributed tremendously to the field.

Siddhidas was born on 2 Bhadra, 1924 BS at Kwachhenni, Keltole of Kathmandu. His father's name was Laxmi Narayan Amatya and his mother's name Harsa Laxmi.

Siddhidas' father was quite poor. So, the family did not have sufficient food and clothes. Siddhidas, therefore, grew in hardship. He had to support his family with different types of wage-winning works he could do.

Siddhidas was keenly interested in learning new things ever since he was a small child. So, he learned the alphabet from his father at home. After he grew up, he went to the family of the rich people of the village to prepare tamakhu— tobacco snuff. As he helped them with their household works, they taught him reading and writing. Gradually, he began to read books available at home. He also learned to write the alphabet properly. His hand-writing was really beautiful. So, simultaneously with his study, he took up the job of a scribe, writing documents at the Accounts Department of Thapathali Palace. His salary was four rupees twelve paisa per month. The income helped him run the course of life in a better way.

At that time, Rarondeep Singh was the Prime Minister of Nepal. Upon his death, Bir Samsher became the Prime Minister. The generals who were stationed in Thapathali Palace where Siddhidas was employed, had been banished from the country by Ranondeep Singh. Siddhidas too lost his job in one hand, and on other, his mother passed away. After the death of his mother, his father married a second wife. The step-mother ignored Siddhidas altogether, and the father took the side of his second wife. Siddhidas was at complete loss now.

The Rana rulers mistreated Newari language very much. Seeing that the Ranas had neglected his mother tongue, Siddhidas' heart was in deep pain. So, he decided to speak and write in his own mother tongue. Seeing not many books in the language, he decided to write books in Newari language. He gradually started expressing his dissatisfaction in poems. Along with poems, he also wrote essays. Writing like this, he prepared many books. A sample of his poem is given here:

Satsanga pauda murkha swata: sajjan bandachha
Padmako patama pani motijhain talpalauchha

[A fool can surely become good or virtuous in the company of the wise. Water shines like pearls on the leaf of lotus.]

Jaaun bhani pad chalaunchha hidchha goda
Au sparsakhatir musardachha haata joda
Ho, rakhnuparchha bashama manako umanga
Ichchha puryauna ma gardina dharmabhanga.

[A mover sets his foot, and the legs carry him forth. To get a touch of something, he stretches his hands. Yes, one should control passion. I don't fall into sin, just to see my desire fulfilled.]

Siddhidas wrote poems but there was no source of income to run his family smoothly. When he grew up, he married a girl named Ganga Devi. After a year, a daughter was born to them. A hard life began, as he now had more responsibility to bear. Even in such a situation, he did not give up writing.

Both of his parents scolded and poked Siddhidas, because he couldn't earn enough. They ruled that serving his mother tongue would not give them any food. However, he never felt like giving up writing.

As he attained newer depths in writing, feelings of patriotism brewed inside him. He thought of starting industries. He began to work in a textile shop. While working there with the spinning threads, he conceived the idea of starting a large fabric industry. He tried for that, but he was threatened by the Ranas. He could not run the project due to the lack of money.

With the help of a friend named Motilal, later on, he went to Birgunj and worked there. Seeing the Newars there, he was worried because they had forgotten their own tongue. He came to realise that writing poems was not sufficient; they needed to be published and broadcasted. So, he collected money and went to Betiya. From there, he published a book named *Sajjanhridayavaran* and sold it out in Birgunj.

After that, in course of work, he went to Calcutta. There, he was further motivated, seeing that the Bengalis published their works in their own language. Excited, he returned with all his manuscripts.

Finding him come back with books instead of money, his parents were furious. However, by the time, he had become a celebrated poet. Without any dealy, he published his books one after another. His published books are as follows:

> **Epic:** 1. Saptastuti, 2. Sajjanhridayavaran, 3. Satya-Sati, 4. Sambad.
> **Long epic:** 1. Siddhi Ramayan.
> **Essay:** 1. Sarva Bandhu.

It is said that books he wrote are more than fifty. But all the books have not been collected.

At the time when Siddhidas was accomplishing literary height, his father, wife, and daughter passed away. He began to stay separately from his step-mother and step-brothers. Looking for a job, he wandered in Kathmandu, and at times in Birgunj and in Calcutta too. At the same time, he caught malaria. No one was there to treat him. His friends had made him get married second time hoping that he would be cared for. But, his new wife showed disregard for him. Quarreling with him on the issue of money, she eloped. Even in such a deplorable situation, he did not stop writing poems.

In the meantime, his health condition worsened day by day. He did not have foodstuff left with him. Then, he began to work in a pharmancy of an Ayurveda doctor. Side by side, he also taught Newari in the Durbar High School.

Again, he fell seriously ill at the age of sixty-three. After his condition grew critical, he was taken to Pashupathi Aryaghat. He died there on 13 Mangsir 1987 BS. A luminary of Newari language and literature, thus, passed away from this world.

■

Jay Prithvi Bahadur Singh: A Pioneer of Children's Literature

Books or writings for children constitute children's literature, and people who contribute to children's literature are called writers of that literature. In Nepal, there were a few writers of children's literature in the past, but today there are plenty. The first writer of Nepali children's literature was Jay Prithvi Bahadur Singh.

Children indeed require different writings or books written for themselves, since they cannot understand books intended for adults. Books for children require lucid and easily understandable language.

Jay Prithvi Bahadur Singh was born at Chainpur of Bajhang District in Seti Zone on 7th Bhadra, 1934 BS. His father Bikram Bahadur Singh was the then king of Bajhang. Everyone loved Prithvi as their own child, though he was the son of a king.

In his childhood, Prithvi watched his father worship gods and goddesses. Carrying that deep impression from his father, he never stopped worshiping in his entire life. He meditated upon God thrice a day—morning, afternoon and evening—and spent an hour in a quiet and peaceful place, every day.

Jay Prithvi Bahadur Singh acquired good habits in his childhood. He adored his parents, learnt to respect his elders and love his juniors. Whenever he saw a beggar, he never walked away without giving alms.

His mother brought Jay Prithvi Bahadur Singh to Kathmandu, when he was only five years old. On the day of his departure from Bajhang, as he was preparing to leave, he saw an old man crying. He approached and asked him the reason for his crying. The old man said, "I am crying because you are leaving us." Wiping his eyes that were full of tears, Jay Prithvi Bahadur Singh assured: "Do not cry. I am going to study so that I will become capable of serving you better." Hearing his soothing words, the old man blessed him profusely.

Then, Jay Prithvi came to Kathmandu. Those days, there was only one school, the Durbar High School. So, he got admitted to that school.

After studying there for some years, he was taken to Calcutta for his higher education. In 1951 BS, he accomplished his matriculation. Since there were no colleges or universities in Nepal and yet he had a strong desire to study further, he went to Prayag, a city in north India, to become a learned man. Like Jay Prithvi Bahadur Singh, any person who wanted to study a lot had no choice but to go to India in those days.

There in India, Jay Prithvi Bahadur Singh studied philosophy, law, and political science etc., and got through his I.A. He also studied a lot of other subjects on his own, without attending university classes.

The then Rana Prime Minister Bir Samsher dethroned Jay Prithvi Bahadur Singh's father to crown Jay Prithvi Bahadur as the King of Bajhang. Jay Prithvi came to Kathmandu for his coronation, and soon returned to Calcutta to complete his education. He came back to Nepal after becoming a learned man.

Jay Prithvi Bahadur Singh married a daughter of the Rana Prime Minister Chandra Samsher in Kathmandu. So, he was now a son-in-law of the Ranas. The Ranas dominated general people in those days; on the contrary, Jay Prithvi always encouraged the people to revolt against all sorts of tyranny and domination. Therefore, he never agreed with the Ranas. Because he was in marital relation with them, they never punished him.

After he returned from India completing his higher education, he went back to Bajhang at the age of 21. He brought some people from Bajhang to Kathmandu, established Satyavadi Prathamik Pathshala, a primary school at his palace in Naxal, and started teaching.

In those days, the government used to publish only one weekly newspaper *The Gorkhapatra* from Kathmandu. The Ranas made Jay Prithvi the Chief Editor of the newspaper. He continued in that post for some years, and then gave it up.

After quitting his job, Jay Prithvi engaged himself in people's education. Thinking that children should study, become knowledgeable and learn good habits, he got some books published for them. He had brought a manual printing press from Calcutta, and with it, he printed books. His activities did not please the Ranas because they never supported any idea of educating the laity. As a result, they started torturing him. Despite all these obstacles, he opened a school in Bajhang as well, built a hospital, hired doctors from India, and made arrangements for the treatment of the sick.

The Ranas tried their best to exploit Jay Prithvi to their advantage, but he did not work for them. Chandra Samsher took him to Britain. Highly impressed by his knowledge and intellect, the British government honored him. On knowing that he was honored by the British government, the Ranas were extremely impatient. They started troubling him even more when he returned to Nepal.

Believing that it was useless to suffer in Nepal, Jay Prithvi wanted to leave his country to stay in India so that he could do his work without any restriction. He abdicated his throne back to his father, and returned to India. Though he settled down in Bangalore building a home, he did not stop working for his country. He opened an organization for humanitarian works, while staying in India.

Jay Prithvi Bahadur Singh wrote altogether 11 books for children. They are:

1. Akshar Mala, 2. Padartha Tatwa Vivek, 3. Shiksha Darpan, 4. Byavhar Mala, 5. Bhugol Vidya, 6. Prakrit Vyakaran, 7. Tatwa Prashamsa, 8. Balbodh (Part I), 9. Balbodh (Part II), 10. Shrestabodh (Part I), 11. Shrestabodh (Part II).

Jay Prithvi Bahadur Singh had written *Akshar Mala* at the age of 14. Soon he got it printed. Other Nepali alphabet book writers imitated it to teach children the alphabet. *Balbodh* part 1 and part 2 too are important books of Nepali children's literature.

Jay Prithvi Bahadur Singh also wrote a grammar of Nepali language. Since there was no such book published in Nepali language before him, he is also known as the first grammarian of Nepali language. Other writers took his grammar as a model to publish grammar books in Nepali language.

Jay Prithvi Bahadur Singh was a resolute follower of truth. He held the conviction that a human being has to work with self motivation and not to follow what others dictate. He taught that everyone in the society should be respected. Everyone should also respect others. There is no superior or inferior human being, and all are equal. For teaching such ideas, he is called a humanistic thinker and writer.

Jay Prithvi Bahadur Singh was very fond of children. He enjoyed a lot when he got an opportunity to play with them. He often stressed that a country should make children wise, bold, and morally upright because they are the future of that nation. He also believed that a good man should serve the poor. He traveled to many countries in order to serve the poor. During those trips, he helped the poor, the war victims and those deprived of education. After some years, Chandra Samsher invited him to stay in Nepal, but he did not return.

Jay Prithvi Bahadur Singh passed away at the age of 63 in Bangalore on 1st of Asoj 1997 BS. Though he is no more with us today, his works of Nepali language and literature and all his commendable deeds will continue to remind Nepali people of his great contributions and sacrifice.

People sacrificing their lives for the betterment of the society never die. Instead, they become immortal. Jay Prithvi Bahadur Singh is also one of such immortal human beings.

■

Linguist Kul Chandra Gautam

Sakala bhutalama talamathi nai
Huna gayo nyayama kali kalale.
Pashupati prabhuka baradanale
Huna gayo Naypala yatharthale.

[In the entire world, both up and down, the spell of Kali started. But, the country called Nepal remained true and unharmed with blessings from Lord Pashupatinath.]

The poet of this above poem is Kul Chandra Gautam. He is also called 'Vidwachhiromani,' the crown of knowledge. He has written many books in Nepali and Sanskrit languages. He had an extraordinary ability of remembering. He could tell anything from fifteen to twenty pages of any book, once he went through it.

Kul Chandra Gautam was born in 1934 BS in Jivanpur village of Dhading District. His father's name was Ramakanta Gautam and his mother's name Hasta Kumari Gautam. He learned the alphabets from his father for the first time.

His *bratabandha*—the initiation rite in Hindu ways—was performed at the age of eight. After that, he went to Banaras and joined school there. After he completed his graduate studies, he also earned a post-graduate degree in Sanskrit literature in the first division from a university there. It is said that he is the first Nepali to complete post-graduation in Sanskrit literature.

He was not satisfied with his post-graduation. He wished to study other subjects, too. So, he re-coursed through various subjects like Vedanta philosophy, treatises, Ayurveda etc.

After he completed his study in Banaras, he came back to Kathmandu. The then King Prithivi Bikram Shah paid him high honor and respect. He then started teaching the book *Dashkumar Charitra* to Prithivi Bikram Shah, the King. At that time, Chandra Samsher was the Prime Minister.

Chandra Samsher had banned teaching that book because the book listed the best virtues of a king, and on learning them, the king would be quite popular, and that would put Rana rule into jeopardy. So, he got angry with Kul Chandra Gautam and termed the book "an insidious one, unfit to teach!" On knowing that, Kul Chandra escaped to Ramnagar of India. He spent quite a long time there as the chief priest at the royal palace. He also passed a long time staying at Janakpurdham, a holy city in Nepal, and Banaras, a holy city in India.

Kul Chandra Gautam wrote poems in Sanskrit ever since he was a child. Later, he began writing poems in Nepali too. His work *Raghawalankar* is one of the great epics in Nepali language. The books he has written are as follows:

In Sanskrit: 1. Bhagawat Manjari, 2. Krishna Karnabharan, 3. Ganga Gaurav, 4. Haribari Vasya, 5. Vandanaayugal, 6. Ayurvediya Yoga.

In Nepali: 1. Purushartha Kalpawalli, 2. Amarkosh, 3. Swayam Vaidya, 4. Alankar Chandrodaya, 5. Dattacharya ra Dattacharya Sarsangraha, 6. Prapanchacharya, 7. Tulasikrit Ramayan, 8. Mahimnastotra, 9. Unmad, 10. Alankar Sangraha, 11. Raghawalankar, 12. Durge Pahi Mam, 13. Loksikha, 14. Tatwabodh, 15. Shiva Mahimnastrotra, 16. Swarnatuladan.

Both in Sanskrit and Nepali: 1. Aadarsha Dampati Sita Ramau.

Amarkosh is a famous book he compiled. The book is assumed to be an extraordinary one because the meanings of so many Sanskrit words have been given in detail in Nepali language, and is a wonderful source of synonyms, better than any other world-class thesaurus.

Once, scholars of Sanskrit language, who assembled in Germany, could not explain a Sanskrit stanza. They sent a letter to many scholars of Nepal and India asking if anyone could explicate the stanza, and furnish an interpretation. The letter came to Kul Chandra Gautam too. He interpreted the stanza, giving thirteen different meanings, and sent it back to Germany. No any other scholars had attempted those many interpretations and meanings of a single stanza. That's why the German Government facilitated him honoring as 'an unequalled scholar.' On knowing that his intellectuality was honored by foreign people, Nepali people were astounded. Only after that Nepalese people felt proud of him because they knew that such an intellect was in Nepal. After that, he was conferred the title of 'Vidwachchhiromani' and awarded with Gorkha Dakshinbahu by the then king, Tribhuvan. The king managed an allowance of three-hundred rupees per month to him until he died.

Kul Chandra Gautam lived in Ramghat, Banaras of India even in his old age. He died in Mangsir, 2015 BS on the day of Krishnaastami, the eighth day of the bright lunar fortnight when Lord Krishna was born. At that time, he was eighty-three years old. All Nepalese people grieved his death thinking that an erudite scholar or a genius had passed away forever.

After a long time following his death, researchers conducted many extensive researches on him. Many scholars of Nepal have written books and articles about him. Such researched books and articles have been published, too. Nepal government has issued a postal stamp with his picture. Mahendra Sanskrit University has published some of his books.

In this way, Kul Chandra Gautam became famous as a legendary hero of Nepal. The Nepalis can never forget him.

■

Nar Bahadur Bharati: The Genius

Nar Bahadur Bharati is a justification of the proverb: "Slow and steady wins the race." A man, who works hard to reach his destination must achieve his goal one day.

Nar Bahadur Bharati is a literary personality, scientist and musician. He is the first man who received the award 'Tribhuvan Pragya Puraskar' after its inception. His ancestral home was at Khopasi of Kavrepalanchok District. His father had come to Kathmandu because their property at Khopasi had been forcefully seized.

Nar Bahadur Bharati was born in 1934 BS in Kamalpokhari, Kathmandu. His father's name was Mahanta Rajeshwar Bharati. After they got their abode and land back in 1970 BS, they returned to Khopasi and stayed there again.

Nar Bahadur Bharati spent his childhood with comfort. He had primarily acquired Sanskrit education according to the norms of those days. Thereafter, he studied English, science and other subjects at home. But he learned so many things in a short passage of time because he was the kind of man who always wanted to learn and know new things.

Nar Bahadur Bharati liked to read and write poems since his very young age. He has written many fine poems. He translated an immortal epic *Kadambari* by Vana Bhatta, a great poet from the neighboring country, India. He contributed immensely to enrich Nepali literature by writing songs and poems. He has written the following books:

1. Kadambari (part 1 and 2 translated from Hindi)
2. Nitisudhar (Jhayaure geet/folk song)
3. Futkar Kabitasangraha
4. Apar Sansar (play in Hindi)

Not only did Nar Bahadur Bharati serve Nepali literature, he also worked hard to usher Nepal into the era of science. He got seriously ill once when he was an adolescent. He suffered from tuberculosis. He became bedridden. Meanwhile, he suffered from different kinds of diseases as a result.

Famous Ayurveda doctors of his days tried to treat him, but his health did not improve. His condition worsened day by day. He did not become nervous, though. For a long time, he took different medicines he prepared himself. He was ultimately cured, and the same disease never appeared in him again.

Nar Bahadur Bharati was also a good Ayurveda doctor. Ayurveda doctors in his days believed that a man couldn't change his destiny, but Bharati proved them wrong by defeating death. The doctors were astounded at what he proved practically.

Bharati also made a kind of homemade rubber from mustard oil. It was inferior in quality to the commercially produced rubber of the modern days, but it could work well like other rubbers.

Once the Rana Prime Minister Chandra Samsher had gone to Mumbai on a special visit. He happened to record his voice on a gramophone, paying sixteen hundred Indian rupees for an hour. When he brought the gramophone to Nepal and explained about it, Nar Bahadur Bharati also got a chance to hear his voice. He was instantly inspired to make something like a gramophone and record his own voice. He started working immediately. It was not an easy task. However, he succeeded because of his incessant effort of day and night.

Though another scientist Gehendra Samsher superseded him in starting a similar work, Bharati got success before the former. The recording device he made was not like that of these days. It was like the bottom of a candle and a pitcher without mouth. That tape-recorder could record and cut the songs and words. Some pieces of splintered recording devices are still in his home at Khopasi in Panauti Municipality of Kavrepalanchok District.

Bharati was a good craftsman too. He made very fine furniture. He also made drums named 'sursringar' and 'bela'. Along with this, he made different items from wood.

Bharati would write songs, compose their music and sing himself. He also played a drum. People from within and outside the country would be delighted seeing the violin he himself manufactured. Along with music, he had a deep interest in painting. He himself drew the pictures for the books he wrote. Some of his fine paintings are still available now.

On 16 Ashad 2016 BS, he was awarded with the title 'Tribhuvan Pragya Puraskar' by Royal Nepal Academy for his praiseworthy and enthusiastic contribution to the field of artistic creation and architecture.

After serving art, music, science and literature in his entire life, he left this world forever on 10 Magha 2023 BS After his death, a postal stamp was issued in his honor. Many research works have been conducted on him. He has become an immortal star of Nepal, always glittering with the light of knowledge and skills.

■

Dramatist Pahalman Singh Swaar

There are many books of dramas in Nepali literature. While reading them, a reader derives great pleasure. Some of them deeply touch the readers. The drama *Atal Bahadur* is that kind of a drama which touches the readers deeply. This play marks the beginning of the tradition of tragic plays in Nepali literature. The drama was published in 1962 BS. It was written by Pahalman Singh Swaar.

Pahalman Singh was born on Monday, 6th of Mangsir 1935 BS at Reedikot of Achham District. His father's name was Laxmi Singh Swaar and mother's name Deekura Devi.

Pahalman was sharp-minded in his early days. He'd like to study, but there were no any schools in Achham. As a result, he read books of Sanskrit and Nepali language available at home, and developed a taste for reading. He studied many books of English and Hindi languages. He did not have any formal certificate of academic qualification. Still, he was a well-educated man. Hence, he wrote many books on different subject matters, and got them published.

Pahalman's father was a government bidder. From a contract he took in 1952 BS, he incurred a heavy loss. Even at that age, the then Rana Prime Minister Bir Samsher decided that bidders should pay fifty thousand rupees to the government from the share of their contract. With this decision, Pahalman's father discontinued taking contracts. His house was seized by the government. When he was still unable to clear-off all debts to the government, an order was announced: "Anyone from Laxmi Singh's famly, who is over sixteen years of age, will be imprisoned."

Laxmi Singh and one of his sons were arrested. But, Pahalman Singh fled to India. He reached a place called Singahi through Lucknow. He stayed in the patronage of Queen Surat Kumari there. While staying there, he began a business, opening an institute named 'L.P. Swaar Company.' During his stay there, he wrote four books *Premamrit Bachan Sangraha, Ankendu Shekhar, Atal Bahadur,* and *Anandaraj.*

Pahalman Singh was keenly interested in sewing and knitting since childhood. At that time, there was a cotton industry in Achham and people prepared garments. Such garments were called 'thetuwa.'

As he came to Kathmandu in 1952 BS, Pahalman saw a kind of textile named 'gharbuna'—home-spun fabric. Immediately, we was interested in learning the art of knitting other types of clothes, besides thetuwa. But, he did not get the opportunity to learn it.

While he was at Singahi, Pahalman Singh observed many factories of garments in Kanpur. Later in 1962 BS, he took training to weave clothes in Gujarat.

In the meantime, he got the news that his mother was sick. By the time, only half of his training had been over. He reached home secretly in Chaitra 1963 BS walking bare foot for ten days through forests and hills. He could be arrested if the Ranas knew about his coming. But nobody knew about his arrival. When he reached home secretly, he knew that his mother had died two months before, father one year and the brother two years back. He went back to India smitten with grief.

At that time, prisoners would be trained to weave clothes at Baroda Jail of India. He too had learned the art of weaving clothes from there. In the same year, knowing that the Rana Prime Minister was coming to Bombay to go to Europe, he reached Bombay. With the help of King Jay Prithvi Bahadur Singh, he met Chandra Samsher and displayed a sample of garments he had prepared. Chandra

Samsher was impressed and freed his family from all accusations. He managed his return to Nepal.

Thereafter, he came to Kathmandu in 1965 BS. There were no any relatives of him in Kathmandu at that time; so he stayed at Jay Prithvi Bahadur Singh's house. Knitting a 'dari'—a kind of carpet made of thick threads—he gave it to Chandra Samsher as a gift. Consequently, he was offered a job to train prisoners in textile weaving.

Pahalman Singh trained prisoners to prepare outfits. He was transferred to the jail of Achham in Bhadra, 1974 BS. As he was there, a case of robbery took place. Taking the incident as a theme, he wrote a book called *Ek Lakh Rupiyako Chori.* He was suspended from his job in Chaitra 1974 BS, because he was accused of helping the prisoners flee.

And then, he worked for other's contract. The contract gave him no profit at all. The loss apart, he was imprisoned in Dillibazaar jail.

Seeing the deplorable condition of the prisoners there, Pahalman wrote a book titled *Khor Rahasya* and sent it to Chandra Samsher. And then, Chandra Samsher became happy with him and freed him from the jail.

Meanwhile, a wedding ceremony was planned for the grandson of Chandra Samsher. Chandra Samsher gave him an assignment to look for a suitable fiance for his grandson. He visited different cities of India.

As he was living in Simla of India, he translated the plays *Ratnawali* and *Avigyan Sakuntal.* On returning from there, he got a job of 'dittha'— a lower-divisional clerk—in the factory of a jail.

Soon he opened Nepal Industry Art Company. He would keep the records of its account. Once, he had to bear some loss because he was unable to sell the goods. So, he was imprisoned again in Bhadra 1989 BS. He was also suspended from his service summarily.

Once Rana Prime Minister Juddha Samsher decided to go for hunting in Kailali and Kanchanpur in 1990 BS. Pahalman got the contract of supplying all the necessary accommodations to the team of hunters. He had bought all the necessary provisions. A heavy earthquake shook the nation on 2nd of Magh, the same year. So, Juddha Samsher immediately returned to Kathmandu. All the provisions Pahalman Singh had bought were wasted. He had to bear a tremendous loss.

Following this incident, he went to Kailali and settled in a village, farming. He wrote other books there.

He wrote many books in his life but didn't publish all of them. Many books of him were posthumously published. His books are as follows:

Plays: 1. Atal Bahadur, 2. Bimala Devi, 3. Laluvaga (First part in Achhami language) 4. Bisnu Maya 5. Jagat Singh.

Poems and Epics: 1. Premamrit Vachan Sangraha, 2. Balopadesh, 3. Premranjan Sringar, 4. Achhamka Chadparba, 5. Khor Rahasya.

Religious Philosophy: 1. Yoga Darshan, 2. Kiskindha Kanda, 3. Pahalman Bhajanmala.

History: 1. Swaarko Kura.

Course Book: 1. Ankendu Shekhar, 2. Katai-Bunai.

Story: 1. Ek Lakh Rupiyako Chori.

Translation: 1. Avigyan Sakuntal, 2. Ratnawali Natika.

Others: 1. Sadar Jelkhanako Niyam, 2. Nepal Udyog Kala Kampanyko Sadharan Niyam, 3. Sadar Jel Karkhanama Baneka ra Banne Maalko Suchipatra, 4. Karsambandhi Ek Sujhab.

In this way, his twenty-three books have been published. Five of his books were lost from the office of Nepal Bhasha Prakashini Samiti. Those books are:

1. Padam Kumari 2. Meghadoot 3. Raghubamsha 4. Jagi Jaginya 5. Laluvaga (part 2).

Apart from this, many other books like *Aanandaraj* are yet to be published.

Beset by numerous pains and difficulties, Pahalman Singh passed away at the age of fifty-six on Sunday, 7th of Jesta, 1991 BS at Pahalmanpur of Kailali District.

Only after a long time of his death, his books began to be published. He was not paid as much respect and homage as he deserved until he was dead. After his death, a postal stamp was issued in his name. Pahalman Library has been opened in Kailali. A literary institution called 'Pahalman Singh Swaar Memorial Foundation' has also been opened. Pahalman Singh Puraskar, a prize, has been instituted in his name, and is distributed to different writers now.

After a long time of his death, he has earned popularity as the first playwright in the field of Nepali tragic plays.

■

Dadhiram Marasini: The Erudite Pundit

Yo chitta suddha navaikana mukti chhaina
Himsa garera mana suddha hudai hudaina.
[There is no salvation, unless the soul is pure. With violence, no one can make his soul pure.]

Sampurna dharmaharooma ta daya chha moola
Tyo moola chhadikana paatabise nabhula.
Bhanchhan sunyau sakal Veda-Purana-shastra
Kati jaro phala chha ke, liyi paata matra.

[Charity is the highest of all virtues. That is the root, and it is worthless to wander around the leaves. If the root is cut, there's no fruit to be availed. This is what the *Vedas*, *Puranas* and the scriputes say.]

These beautiful lines have been written by Dadhiram Marasini, a great scholar of Nepal. He is also equally renowned as a great pundit. He is both a literary figure and an educationist.

Dadhiram was born on the day of Ashad Suklaastami—the eighth day of the bright fortnight—in 1939 BS at Khidim-Pokharathok in Aarghakhanchi District. His father's name was Parichit Marasini and his mother's name Khageshwari. His mother died three years after Dadhiram was born. So he was brought up by his grandmother.

Dadhiram learned the alphabets from his father at the age of five. He read some Sanskrit books at home. He stared his formal education in Pokhara of Kaski District after his *bratabandha*—Hindu rite of initiation for a boy—was performed at the age of eight. And then, he studied at Patan Devi Sanskrit School at Tulasipur of India. He acquired the degree of Prathama, the first school examination in Sanskrit, in the first division from there in 1956 BS. He had more passion for studying. So, he came to Kathmandu and joined the Royal Sanskrit School at Ranipokhari. He studied there till 1959 BS. Kavisiromani Leknath Paudyal—the great poet—was his close friend.

After his study there, he went to Banaras of India, where he got through the intermediate degree in grammar in the first division from Royal Sanskrit College in 1961 BS.

Lekhnath Paudyal had advised him to stay in Kathmandu. But he returned to his own village Khidim with an objective of spreading the light of education to the village folks. During his stay in the village, he got married at the age of twenty-one.

Dadhiram started teaching free of charge at his own home. After the number of students increased, he began teaching at the local Dashain-house in 1974 BS. Later, he got Harihar Gautam, a friend of him, to open schools in his own direction at Harrabot and Malika in 1985 BS and 1989 BS, respectively. Harihar Gautam also opened Harihar Sanskrit School according to the direction of Dadhiram. Dadhiram started teaching there free of charge. Students he had taught held respected posts and positions, and became famous in their lives.

Dadhiram wrote poems since his schooldays. He could write beautifully both in Sanskrit and Nepali languages. During student life, a kind of competition would always continue between Lekhnath and Dadhiram in writing poems. In his support, Lekhnath had written beautiful poems. Some published books of Dadhiram are as follows:

In Nepali: 1. Sadupadesh, 2. Bhaktibilas, 3. Shri Krisnadbhut Charitam, 4. Shri Ramkripalahari,

5. Bishnumanas Puja, 6. Shivastuti, 7. Kashi Biraha, 8. Bhagawati Mahima, 9. Bhasmastakam, 10. Pran Vichar, 11. Surya Narayan Stuti, 12. Kal Samrajyam, 13. Gangastrotra. **In Sanskrit language:** 1. Shri Ram Charitamritam, 2. Shri Krishna Charitramritam, 3. Satwamala, 4. Karmakanda Bhashkar, 5. Antyakarma Paddhati.

Apart from these, he has written *Sukla Yajurveda* in forty different sections, and important books like *Srimadvagawat Geeta* and *Durga Saptasati* in beautiful hand-script in *Nepali kagaj*—indigenous Nepali paper, manually manufactured.

Dadhiram Marasini, a great pundit of Nepal, died at the age of eighty-two on 23 Chaitra 2020 BS in Benaras of India. After his death, all Nepalese people felt that they had lost a great legend, who was ever committed to scattering the light of knowledge in the field of Nepali academia and literature. His books *Gangastotra* and a collection of books named *Nepali Bhasaslok Sangraha* were posthumously published in 2021 BS.

Harihar Sanskrit School founded by Dadhiram Marasini, was taken over by Mahendra Sanskrit University itself in 2055 BS. In honor of Dadhiram, the government issued a postal stamp. In his commemoration, an institution named 'Dadhiram Marasini Smirti Pratisthan' has been established and an anthology named *Mahapundit Dadhiram Marasini Smirti Grantha* in more than eight hundred pages, has been published by the very institution in 2060 BS. His poems have been collected in a book. Many researches have been conducted about him. Scholars have acquired the degrees of Doctor of Philosophy (PhD) for their research on his works and life.

Scholars like Dadhiram Marasini are seldom born in this world. He is a great legend of Nepal.

Litterateur Rammani Acharya Dixit

Many linguists and litterateurs have contributed immensely to enrich Nepali language and literature. Out of them, Rammani Acharya Dixit—popularly called Rammani AaDi—is one. 'Acharya' is his surname, and 'Dixit' his title. The family name 'AaDi' has continued as a combination of the two.

Rammani was born in the month of Chaitra, on Krishnapakchha Pratipada Day—the first day after the full moon night in Chaitra in 1939 BS at Pandhiki, Tukucha Kathmandu. His father's name was Kashinath and mother's name Lalita Devi. His name, given at the name-giving ceremony was Rameshwar Prasad, but later, it was changed to Rammani.

Rammani learned the alphabet and started reading Sanskrit at home. Later on, he went to Banaras of India with his grandfather. There, he passed Prathama, the first examination in Sanskrit in the first division. In 1956 BS, he joined the Queen's College in Banaras. He received five rupees per month as scholarship there. He passed his intermediate from there and later on completed his graduation. He continued his higher studies through post-graduation. His major was English.

Rammani tied his knot of marriage with Kumudini Devi at the age of thirteen in 1952 BS. He got married with Nalini Devi second time in 1969 BS after his first wife died in 1968 BS.

In early 1957 BS, Rammani had come to Kathmandu from Banaras. He was appointed as a scribe to the then commander-in-chief Bhim Samsher since Mangsir, 1957

BS. At that time, his salary was eight hundred rupees, annually. He quit that job in 1960 BS because Bhim Samsher did not like him. He went back to Banaras thereafter.

A printing press named 'Pravakari Mudranalaya' had been founded in partnership with his uncle previously there. He worked at that printing press. After he started working there, more books of Nepali language were published. He led a new movement 'Halanta Bahishkar Andolan' in the field of Nepali language at the time. It was a movement to reject *halanta*—a punctuation appended at the end of consonant letters to indicate that they are pronounced without the terminal vowels. Their argument was that such a thing was unnecessary.

Rammani started writing prose works because poems had many practitioners as that was the most dominant mode but there were few who professed prose. In his effort, Nepali was introduced as a compulsory subject in the high schools in Benaras, India. Course books were printed in his press. Besides printing books, he began publishing a monthly magazine called *Madhavi* in Kartik, 1965 BS with an objective to making Nepali prose even more popular. 'Matrika Prasad Sharma' was the name that featured as its editor, though the name was a pseudonym of Rammani himself. He collected eight thousand Nepali words to compile a Nepali dictionary while printing *Madhavi*.

Rammani was called back to Kathmandu in Bhadra 1966 BS because Chandra Samsher thought that if he stayed in Banaras, Rana regime would be at stake. Since Kartik, he started working in the treasury of King Prithivi Bikram Shah. Chandra Samsher sent him to work in Singha Durbar in 1970 BS, because he was dear to the King. He became 'Mir Subba' – an official post beneath section officer, after a promotion. In Falgun 1970 BS, he established an institution named 'Gorkha Bhasa Prakashini Samiti' under his own chairmanship. He remained its chairman for nineteen years.

Rammani wrote many books and translated some. He translated a Sanskrit book *Madhavnidhan* in 1953 BS, but the book was lost before it got published.

Rammani had written dairies too during his life time. He had written daily notes in thirty-five copies. Among them, some of the dairies have been published, though some daily notes are yet to be published. Books he has written are these:

Written books: 1. Sadharan Chaltiko Aushadhi, 2. Rogiko Paricharya Athawa Syaharsusar-Sambhar, 3. Bhalo Kurako Namuna, 4. Ek Samiksha, 5. Matriboliko Swang, 6. Matribhasa, 7. Ukhan Sangraha, 8. Purano Samjana, 9. Samjhanako Batoma, 10. Yatra Sansmaran.

Translated books: 1. Madhav Nidan (Manuscript lost), 2. Safalta ra tyo Sadhne Upaya, 3. Kartavyata Parichaya.

Unpublished books: 1. Manikosh, 2. Bhool, 3. Nitiko Upadesh, 4. Manikhalakko Katha, 5. Bhasa ra Vyakaran, 6. Nitiko Petaro.

Rammani opened Shantiniketan Library at his own home in 1966 BS. He worked as the officer-in-charge with the Earthquake Victim Rescue Council from 1990 to 1996 BS. He also worked in the Council of Constitution Improvisation from 2003 to 2008. He became a sardar in 2005 BS, but left the job in 2008 BS.

Rammani was rendered imbecile by paralysis in 2021 BS due to high blood pressure. Thereafter, he was confined to bed. He died at the age of eighty-nine on 23 Magh, 2028 BS in Kathmandu. After his death, many writers of Nepal wrote about him. A book named *Rammani AaDi: Byakti ra Kriti* has been published in his memory. In his honor, a postal stamp has been issued. His name will be remembered forever through his works of art.

■

Chakrapani Chalise: The Gifted Author

Arkakai bharama chha bilkula khupi
    aaphu maha sunya chha
Ichchha rakchha karodako jiu bhane
    aalasyako daasa chha.
Dilli haktachha jodidinchha gaphale
    aakasha-patala nai
Surojhain aghi sarna khojchha
    ranama tau jungama didai.

[The stanza tells, the ability of a man is zero if he depends so much on others. His lazy body craves for billion of rupees. He claims to seize Delhi, or the sky and the underworld, and like a grave soldier, fiengs to make advances oiling his moustache.]

The above verses were written by Chakrapani Chalise. In 2021 BS, Tribhuvan Puraskar had been conferred on Chakrapani Chalise, often called the Vyas of Nepali prose literature, comparing him with the complier of the *Mahabharata* and *Bhagavata Purana*, for, he worked for Nepali literature all his life with unprecedented commitments. Such an award conferred after one is dead is called 'Maranoparanta' or 'Posthumous' award.

Chalise was born in 1940 B.S in Katunje of Bhaktapur. His father was Premlal—a dittha, or a lower division clerk—and his mother, Chandra Maya.

Chalise has introduced himself and his family in a piece of poem:

Chalise thar ho gharai chha bujhanu gaun
    Katunjemaha
Mero naama chha Chakrapani ma ta chhu Sri
    Kantipurma yaha.

[I belong to the Chalise family, and I am from Katunje. My name is Chakrapani, and I live in the Kantipur valley.]

Chalise cleared his Madhyama, equivalent to intermediate degree in Sankskrit, and Sahityatirtha in grammar. He deeply loved his mother tongue ever since he was a student. He began publishing articles in a magazine called *Sundari* published from Banaras. He also became the sub-editor of that magazine later. Thus, he started working for literature since his student days.

After completing his studies, he had to engage in a job for his livelihood. He worked at Gorkha Bhasha Prakasani Samiti (later Nepali Bhasha Prakasani Samiti) since 1970 BS and at *Gorkhapatra* since 1998 BS.

The books written by Chakrapani, a genius of prose, are as follows:

Prose: 1. Samchhipta Ramayan, 2. Samchhipta Mahabharat, 3. Jaimani Bharat, 4. Gorkha Siksha, 5. Patrabodh, 6. Dharma Siksha, 7. Sahitya-Mimamsa, 8. Prabandha Rachana Siksha, etc.

Verse: 1. Stotrawali, 2. Machhindranathko Katha ra Thuprai Varnik Chhandaka Kavitaharoo.

Dictionaries: 1. Bagali Kosh, 2. Paryayavachi Sabdakosh etc.

Thus, a writer of many books in Nepali language, Chalise occupies a prominent place in the history of Nepali literature. Before the declaration of republic, Nepal's national anthem was 'Shriman Gambhir Nepali.' The anthem had been composed by him.

Laxmi Nandan Chalise, his son, was convicted with a treachery case by the Rana government. He became as eyesore for the rulers. So, he was rusticated from the school and imprisoned for four years. His entire property was seized. That was returned later. But, he died in 2002 BS in jail.

The death of his son hurt Chalise deeply. He also had to bear the grief of his wife's untimely death. Then, he became restless because of the family sorrow.

Ultimately, he took retirement from service. Even at the of 70, he resumed his studies for subsistence. His condition turned worse day by day because of oldness and poverty.

Seeing such a situation, an allowance of 150 rupees per month was offered by the state. Eventually, one of the hardworking and strong poets and writers of Nepali literature passed away in 2014 BS.

After his death, he was honored with Tribhuvan Puraskar by Royal Nepal Academy for his worthy contribution to Nepali literature.

■

Punditraj Somanath Sigdel

*Sikskya-sudha komala baalakaima
Bhijdai gai chaldachha
    chittachalma.
Chhatinchha aalo biruwa jaso gari
Jhaginchha, sojhinchha, nuhunchha
    so sari.
Rakshya gari komala halahalako
Siksya khulyo layak kalakalako.*

[Education is an elixir for the young mind, which extends its roots in the heart. Like a young plant growing, a well-educated mind grows in virtues. Education, that saves the nuanaces of a time, helps people of every age.]

These verses were written by Poet Somanath Sigdel who is popular in Nepali literature as 'Punditraj'.

Somanath Sigdel was born in Ashwin, 1941 BS in Kathmandu. He not only had excellent knowledge of Sanskrit language, but also was an expert of the *Vedas* written in Sanskrit, the *Upanishads*, the theological portion of the *Vedas*, and other works of Sanskrit literature, Nepali literature, and grammar. For this erudition, he received the title of 'Punditraj', meaning, a great scholar.

Somanath's father's name was Jagannath Upadhyaya and mother's Laxmi Lila Devi. As the saying goes 'hune biruwako chillo pat' —*morning shows the day*—Somanath was sharp-minded since a very young age. He received his primary education from Nepal Pradhan Sanskrit School. Then, he went to Banaras for higher education. He became a first-class student in studies even there. He always upheld the esteem and prestige of Nepali students.

He initially wrote poems in Sanskrit. He later began to write in Nepali deciding to work for Nepali language and literature. Some of the books he wrote are these:

1. Aadarsha Raghav, 2. Laghu Chandrika, 3. Sahitya Pradeep, 4. Upadesh Satak, 5. Madhya Chandrika, 6. Anubad Chandrika, 7. Sanskrit Chandrika and so on.

Many of his books are yet to be published.

Somanath worked for many years as a teacher and principal. Yet, he along side worked for literature. Although he was an erudite man of Sanskrit, he showed his flair equally well in Nepali. It was a great characteristic in him. Though a lot of Sanskrit vocabulary has mixed up with his Nepali composition, senses are explicit. For example:

Ram Chandra abatirna hundama
Kanti-shanti bhariyi janatama.
Andhakara manako pani bhagyo
Harshako udadhi urlana lagyo.

[When Ram Chandra was born
Glory and peace filled among the people;
Darkness of the mind receded far
Oceans of joy rippled and roared.]

Articles and creations of Punditraj are the kinds which touch the heart of ordinary people. He says, a poem should be patterned in rhyme by virtue of which it becomes easy to read and comprehend. He served the country and its people not only by writing literature, but also by writing books, grammar and dictionaries. He has greatly contributed to Nepali language and literature.

Even after he retired from teaching, he did not remain passive. Becoming the member of Royal Nepal Academy, he ceaselessly worked for his country and literature. He was given Tribhuvan Puraskar in 2024 BS as a mark of recognition for his work.

How much important his labor and services are to literature can be known from the titles, honors, medals, adornments, and prizes he won. Numerous readers and students of Punditraj Sigdel are the proof of the same.

The life of Somnath, who enriched in the beautiful garden of literature, ended in 2029 BS. His invaluable works have still lived and will live forever. In fact, he was a philosopher, poet, grammarian, and scholar of Nepal. He is immortal in the heart of Nepali people as a decent professor, dear guru, and rightful heir of religious science as well as the best poet of Nepal.

■

Lekhanath Paudyal : The Crown of Poets

Balak baburo dwija suka nama
Hoon ma pareko chhu pinjarama.

[A baby-parrot I am; they call me 'dwija'. I am caught in a cage.]

Do you know who wrote this timeless song? If not, I tell you. His name is Kavi Shiromani—the Crown of Poets—Lekhanath Paudyal. He was born in 1941 BS in the month of Poush in a village called Arghaun-Aarchale, in Kaski District of Gandaki Zone. His father's name was Durgadatta and his mother's name Basundhara.

Lekhanath became attracted to reading and writing at an early age. He read many books at home. He started writing beautiful poems in Nepali language since childhood. Some people, who would despise his poems at the time, began to praise him later on.

There were no any schools in his village at the time. One had to go either to Pokhara or Kathmandu in order to study. At the time, the name of 'Kashi' and 'Kaski' were famous for education. After completing his study from a school of Kaski, the poet came to Kathmandu and joined Tindhara Sanskrit School.

Lekhanath wrote poems in Sanskrit too. He published many of his poems in a literary magazine *Suktisudha* published from Kashi. He also got some of them published in *Sundari*, a monthly Nepali, published from Kashi. By 1963 BS, the magazine *Sundari* had become quite popular among poets.

Lekhanath returned to Kathmandu after completing his study in India. Here, he looked for a job. He got a job of teaching children of the then Prime Minister Bhim Samsher. Considering the activities of his surroundings, he wrote a famous poem named "Pinjarako Suga"—A Parrot in the Cage—at the same time.

Lekhanath has given us many books we need to read, and books that enrich our knowledge and wisdom. His main works of epics and poems are:

1. Lalitya (Parts I and II), 2. Buddhi Binod, 3. Ritu Vichar, 4. Satya-Kali Samvad, 5. Mero Ram, 6. Tarun Tapasi, 7. Ganga-Gauri and, 8. Laxmi Puja, a play.

Three works of translation to his credit are Panchatantra, Avigyan Sakuntal and Vatrihari Nirveda.

The poems he has written are easy to understand and well-crafted. For instance:

Kaha thiyo baasa aghi ma ko thiyen
Kaso hunda yo pinjara lindo bhayen.
Kaha chha jaanu kuna saatha lieekana
Talai malum chha ki yo kura mana.

[O, where was my retreat and who was I earlier? What made me reach this cage? Where am I to go now, and in whose company? Do you know all these things?]

Since his poems and works are extremely beautiful, Lekhanath was given the title 'Kavi Shiromani'—the Crown of Poets—by the nation with a great honor in 2008 BS. In 2011 BS, he was given a chariot ride to honor him in Kathmandu. General people of the country as well as other poets paid due respect to him. His Majesty's government gave him Rs. 5000 as a cash prize because he had made Nepali language and literature stronger, more attractive, refined and beautiful.

Besides this, Lekhanath got 'Tribhuvan Puraskar' in 2026 BS. He worked as a member of Royal Nepal Academy since its inception. He became a full-time member of this institution as well.

Lekhanath fell seriously ill in 2022 BS. In the belief that if one died in Kashi, he would get redemption, he was taken to Kashi. He fell into consciousness on the way. So, he was taken to Devghat of Nepal, not Kashi of India, as he had willed.

He passed away in the holy pilgrimage site of Devghat.

Lekhanath's works have been disseminated everywhere. A God-blessed soul he was, our poet Kavi Shiromani Lekhanath Paudyal.

■

Krishna Lal Adhikari: A Literary Martyr

Krishna Lal Adhikari is the first literary martyr of Nepal. He is Nepal's first litterateur to be jailed, and left to die in prison, for writing a book. Hence, his name will always be remembered by the readers of Nepali literature.

Krishna Lal was born on Magha, Sukla Ekadasi Day—the eleventh day in the bright fortnight—in 1944 BS. His father's name was Laxman Adhikari and mother's name Indra Kumari. Krishna Lal was the second of the seven sons of his parents. His birth place was Kathjhor of Ramechhap District. At that time, if one liked to study, Sanskrit was the only option. So, Krishna Lal learned the alphabet at the age of five, and began reading Sanskrit. His *bratabandha*—initiation rite of the Hindu boys—was performed when he was eight years old. After that, he began reading many Sanskrit books.

There was a village named Chatauna, north of Gaur, the district headquarters of Rautahat District. The village was called 'Chataunagar' previously. There was an office that dealt in timber with India. Chandra Lal Adhikari, Krishna Lal's father's second elder brother, was the official in-charge in the office.

Krishna Lal's father took Krishna Lal to Chatauna and left his son with his brother. Krishna Lal's father had an understanding that his son would read and write well and get an attractive job in the future. Staying at Chatauna, Krishna Lal read a lot. He also got a job at his uncle's office after reading till sixteen years.

At that time, there was a palace of Rana Prime Minister Chandra Samsher, near Chatauna. The palace was called 'Hajmaniya Durbar.' Chandra Samsher used to stay there to escape the biting cold of the months of Mangsir, Paush, and Magh. He used to go for hunting and invite foreigners to accompany him in hunting.

Those days, a person who could write petitions as cleanly and correctly as possible and brief Chandra Samsher, was being looked for, because he had to answer the people's complaints. Krishna Lal had a wonderful writing capacity, because he had read Sanskrit and his handwriting was clean and beautiful.

Chandra Lal took the boy to Hajmaniya Durbar as a candidate for the job. There, Krishna Lal was examined. He passed the examination and started to work as a typist. Chandra Samsher was quite happy with his performance.

After some time, Chandra Samsher sent Krishna Lal to Kathmandu. He was given a job at a wood store in Naksal. After some time, he was promoted to dittha—an official rank below subba—to help the Prime Minister listen to petitions at Niksari Adda, a local court. After he worked there for four years, he was again promoted. He became a nayab subba—a non-gazetted officer of a clerical rank. Thereafter, people called him 'Subba Saheb'.

People had started talking against Rana regime by then. The Ranas were being flayed in the undercurrent movements, although people could not talk against them on the surface. Krishna Lal had also begun to be an opponent of the Ranas. The thought that people should unite and go against Rana's regime struck his mind. But it was a really risky task to resist the Ranas while holding a job at one of their offices. So, he thought to oppose the Ranas by writing a book. He thought that if he wrote double-meaning sentences, he could escape the penalty by interpreting it in ways different from the one the Rana's would receive it as. So, he began writing the book *Makaiko Kheti*—meaning 'the maize field'.

The book mentioned *rata-tauke kira* and *kala-tauke kira*—red-headed worms and black-headed worms—as worms that attack the maize crop. At that time, Chandra Samsher used to wear a red hat on his head and Bhim Samsher a black one. So, wise men sensed the book's resistive satire against Chandra Samsher and Bhim Samsher. A section of the book runs like this in paraphrase:

'Since a British dog, living with happiness and comfort, is unable to protect the maize field, a Nepali dog is in demand for its safety.'

During that time, the Ranas had been ruling in Nepal at the mercy of the British. Thus, the meaning was obviously made out: British dog was the government of the British in India and Nepali dog, the Rana government of Nepal which was patronized by the British rulers in India.

People do not have to go far to earn enemies. A trusted man can turn an enemy with the passage of time. Krishna Lal disputed with his own relative Ram Chandra Adhikari on a land issue. The danger involved in the tussle was that, if Ram Chandra disclosed the hidden meaning of Krishna Lal's book to the Ranas, Krishna Lal would be thrown to the jail.

As the dispute aggravated, the worst came about. Ram Chandra Adhikari leaked the secret of the book to the Ranas, thinking that he would get a job and award from the rulers and also get the larger portion of the disputed land. As a consequence, Krishna Lal was arrested on 10 Shrawan 1977 BS.

Those days, one could not publish a book without the approval of the Gorkha Bhasha Prakasani Samiti. On hearing that Krishna Lal had penned a book, Mohan Samsher had given the permission to print it. But on knowing that the book had anti-Rana issues, all its copies were collected back. Nine hundred and nineteen copies of the book were retrieved. But one copy was still missing. All the books collected like that were burnt in a bonfire. Krishna

Lal was sentenced to three years' imprisonment. He was also sentenced for extra three years because the lost book was not found. Krishna Lal became a prisoner.

Chandra Samsher loved Krishna Lal very much. So, he sent a message that he might be acquitted if he confessed his mistake. But, not an inch did Krishna Lal retract from his belief. He did not beg for excuse. Thus, he became a jaibird.

Inside the jail, he was attacked by tuberculosis. Eventually, he died on the day of shukla tritiya—third day of the bright fortnight—in the month of Magha, in 1990 BS, his hands still carrying the manacles.

After his death, a manuscript he had written long back was retrieved, and published with the title *Dharmakumari Shiksha*. This way, his creations numbered to two:
1. Makaiko Kheti, 2. Dharmakumari Siksha.

Krishna Lal Adhikari has become a source of inspiration for literary figures across Nepal as a revolutionary warrior. Many research works have been conducted on him and his works. Books have been published, too. One of the main things is that he will remain in the hearts of the Nepalese people as long as Nepal, Nepali language and Nepali literature survive.

■

Baburam Acharya : The Great Historian

Baburam Acharya, the great historian, was born at Sinamangal in Kathmandu on 29th Falgun 1944 BS. Today, the Tribhuvan International Airport is situated in that place.

Baburam was born of father Dharmadatta Acharya and mother Shivkumari Acharya. The title 'Itihas Shiromani'—the Greatest Historian—has been conferred on him because he possessed unmatched knowledge of history.

Baburam's father was a great scholar of Sanskrit. He taught his son Sanskrit since childhood. As a child, Baburam was very keen in studies. His memory power was extraordinary. At first, his father wanted to get him admitted to Durbar High School so that he could learn English. But he failed to have him enrolled there. After this, Baburam was admitted to Ranipokhari Sanskrit Pathshala, and he completed his primary education from that school.

Baburam set out for Banaras in India for his higher education at the age of seventeen. It so happened that he could not stay there to complete his study, but in a short period of two years he passed there, he studied astrology, theology and grammar. Then, he returned home.

After coming back to Kathmandu, he thought of taking up a job to earn his living. According to the rules and regulation of that time, any person who stood first in a competitive examination could receive a job at a government office. He appeared at one of such examinations, and topped.

Accordingly, he was appointed kharidar, a clerk, in 1967 BS. However, he left the job in 1976 BS because of his declining health condition. He also received another blow when his father expired in the same year. Whatever misfortunes befell him, he was not a man to give in and become despondent. As time passed, he recovered from sickness. Again, he got appointed to the position of kharidar exactly after one year. He worked in the same post for thirty-one years and retired in 1998 BS.

There is an interesting event describing how Baburam Acharya involved himself in digging out history. The event occurred in 1976 BS. In Hindu ritual and custom of cremation, the remains, especially small pieces of bones, are ritually disposed in a great river like the Ganges.

When his father died, Baburam went to the River Ganges in India to perform the final ritual of his father's body. He had read in a book about ancient scriptures at a place called Ara in Bihar State in India. He was tempted to see the stone carvings of Lichchhavi King Jaydev, about which, he had read in the book. He developed a keen interest to explore the ancient history of Nepal and get it published.

Having made an unshakable determination, he devoted himself to the exploration of stone carvings, documents engraved on copper plates and palm leaves, and genealogy. In the course of time, his inclination towards history deepened.

Those days, ancient books about Nepal were stored at Bir Pustakalaya, a library in Kathmandu. Reading extensively in the library, Baburam went on thinking deeply about ancient history. His eyesight declined, as he read for hours the dim and faded letters on stone carvings, documents on copper plates and palm leaves, and other old documents. Despite all these, he was not to be discouraged. In the end, he grew completely blind, but continued the exploration of history till the end of his life.

The list of books written by the great historian Baburam Acharaya includes:

1. Purana Kavi ra Kavita, 2. Tulanatmak Sundarkanda, 3. Nepalko Shamshipta Britanta, 4. Shree Paanch Badamaharajdhiraj Prithivi Narayan Shahko Samshipta Jeevani (published in four volumes).

In addition to these books, his writings on Nepali language, literature, culture, and history have been published in different magazines and newspapers. The book *Aba Yasto Kahilyei Nahos* was published after his death.

His untiring devotion to the exploration of history was first duly recognized in 2008 BS when King Tribhuvan conferred on him the title 'Itihas Shiromani', the greatest historian. Following this, Royal Nepal Academy honored him with Tribhuvan Puraskar for his special contribution to Nepali history. He was also honored with Gorkha Dakshinbahu in 2028 BS. Furthermore, he was privileged to have the honorary membership of the Royal Nepal Academy for life. Thus, he was honored by his country.

Eventually, working assiduously and relentlessly, he went to his heavenly abode at the age of 85 on 21st Bhadra 2029 BS.

■

Educationist Basudev Bhattarai

People remember the name of Basudev Bhattarai with due reverence. He is an exponent in various fields, including literature, history, education, religion and culture. He is one of the greatest intellectual figures of Nepal. He taught for forty years at a school. He translated religious books into Nepali from Sanskrit. He wrote books of history and also edited  others' writing. Profoundly renowned luminaries like Bal Krishna Sama and Keshar Bahadur K.C. were his pupils. He is, therefore, an extraordinary personality of Nepal.

Basudev Bhattarai was born on 24 Baishak 1945 BS in Banaras of India. His parents' were Mohandatta Bhattarai and Menaka Devi. In Banaras, Mohandatta taught at a school and during one of those days, Basudev was born as his youngest son. At birth, the child was named Yagyeshwar. He was a mulyaha—his constellation at the time of birth being *mula*—considered to be problematic. There was a belief that such a child should not be raised by the parents themselves. Therefore, he grew at his uncle's house.

At his uncle's house, he started his primary education in English and Sanskrit languages. His wedding party was also performed at his uncle's house. He got married to Bhuwaneshawri Devkota. By then, he had completed his B.A. Soon after, he came to Kathmandu quitting his teaching job in Banaras.

It is an incident of 1973 BS. Nepal was under the rule of the Ranas, and Chandra Samsher was the Prime Minister, then. Except Tri-Chandra College and Durbar High School, there were no other schools in Kathmandu Valley. Literate scholars were also quite a few. After Durbar High School introduced Nepali subject in its course of study there was a necessity of a teacher who could teach the subject. Hearing that Basudev Bhattarai was a scholar, Chandra Samsher sent his chief official Marichman to Banaras to fetch Basudev into Nepal. Marichman brought Basudev into Nepal. Later, his wife and children also came selling their properties away. Basudev started teaching Nepali at Durbar High School.

After Juddha Samsher became the Prime Minister, he made an increment of two hundred rupees in Basudev's monthly salary. Later he was requested to be *badahakim*— the chief officer of the district administration. But becoming a teacher, he thought, was a more fascinating job. So he rejected the offer. Mohan Samsher used to call him 'man of steel' because of his fearless nature. He had earned much fame as a 'strict-natured master' for his strict treatment even to the children of the Ranas, who used to come to study with him, even at a time when the Ranas were ruling the country.

In 1991 BS, a literary magazine named *Sharada* started getting published. Writers who contributed their writings for it, gathered at his home and discussed about their writing. His relationship with those writers like Siddhi Charan Shrestha, Bal Krishna Sama, Puskar Samsher, Baburam Acharya, and Surya Bikram Gyawali was well-established. Basudev who had inspired, and helped writers by sharing this experiences, was the main source of inspiration for Surya Bikram Gyawali later for his book *Prithivi Narayan Shah*.

After teaching at Durbar High School for many years, Basudev Bhattarai joined Padmakanya Vidyashram as a teacher. He served there for forty years. People often called him 'Master Baje' with respect, while others called him 'Bhattarai Baje', and some others 'Madsab'. He taught till 2012 BS.

Finding that there were quite a few books of history in Nepali language, he himself wrote some history books. That was during the time of Rana regime. For writing a book, he got two hundred and fifty rupees cash-prize from Juddha Samsher. Apart from this, he also translated two Sanskrit works into Nepali language, which were considered to be influential in the field of religious and cultural studies. His works made him immortal. His works are these:

History: 1. Bharatbarsako Itihas (Purbardha), 2. Bharatbarsako Itihas (Uttarardha), 3. England ko Itihas.

Translation: 1. Srimad Valmikiya Ramayan, 2. Maharshi Veda Vyaspranit Srimadvagawat Mahapuran (first part), 3. Maharshi Veda Vyaspranita Srimadvagawat Mahapuran (second part).

Out of these books, three had been printed during Rana times. The translated version of *Ramayana* was printed in 1997 BS. Its second edition came in 2022 BS. The first part of *Srimadvagawat* was printed in 2017 BS, and the second part in 2020 BS.

Basudev Bhattarai did not remain idle, although he took retirement in 2012 BS. For seventeen years following his retirement, he continued reading different kinds of books. He was quite fond of reading. If he found any books written in Nepali, English or Hindi, he would not leave them without reading.

Staying at Battutole of Kathmandu, he built a house at Jhamsikhel of Latitpur District and moved there. In the last years of his life, he walked on foot for three hours in the morning up to Pashupathinath from Jhamsikhel because he had to control hyper tension from which he was suffering.

Basudev Bhattarai became bed-ridden and unconscious in 2029 BS. He was taken to Bir Hospital. After he didn't come back to consciousness, he was taken to Pashupathi Aryaghat—a holy cremation spot on the bank of the holy Bagmati River in Kathmandu, as per the advice of the doctors.

After six days, he came into consciousness, and he was taken back to his home. Later on in Kartik, he was again attacked by the same problem. He was taken to Shanta Bhawan Hospital. After checking him up, doctors advised the family members to take him to Pashupathi Aryaghat again. He was taken there, accordingly. Ten hours later, he passed away at four o'clock in the morning on Kartik 16, 2020 BS, on the eleventh day of the lunar fortnight. He was eighty-four at that time.

The country soaked in tears at his death. Everyone paid homage at the demise of Nepal's dignified teacher, worthy man, fearless guru, religious litterateur, translator, and historian.

Basudev Bhattarai was an ideal personality of Nepal. Nepal lost a great scholar at his demise. His works are with us even if he is dead. A book has been published in his remembrance. Researches have been conducted on him.

Basudev Bhattarai will be living in our hearts as an ideal and an inspiring personality for many generations in future.

■

Shambhu Prasad Dhungel:
A Gifted Poet

Janchhin aaja Shakuntala ghara
   bhani uthto chha chinta ati
Pritika manama prabaha bahanda
   rokinna aansu rati
Hami jhai banabasiko pani bhayo
   yo gat bhane yo ghadi
Baschhan dhairya gari grihastha
   kasari chhori bidai gari.

[Knowing that Shakuntala was leaving for her own husband's home, her father grew extremely forlorn, and tears flowed prodigally. When the near ones are touched so deeply, one can never stop tears. If, those of us who lived in the vicinity of her ashram in the forest, were so deeply pained, one can imagine how a father stayed back seeing his beloved daughter off.]

The poet who wrote such beautiful verses was none but Shambhu Prasad Dungel. He was born in 1946 BS at Bhatbhateni of Kathmandu, on the day of Krishna Pakhsha Ekadasi, the first day of dark fortnight in the month of Chaitra. His father's name was Devi Raman Upadhyaya Dungel.

Poet Dhungel was quite a genius. He had passed Madhyama—intermediate equivalent—in Sanskrit. Soon he discovered his poetic powers. He could compose poems on any subject in any rhyme any time.

One day, he happened to reach Singha Durbar. Chandra Samsher was the Prime Minister of Nepal at the time. Standing in front of the Prime Minister, he showed his greeting. Someone told that he was a poet. Chandra Samsher said, "If you are a poet, recite a poem describing the upper part of this palace."

Looking at the upper part of the palace, he recited a poem in rhymes there and then. A rhymed poem is one which can be read in a musical tone. Seeing him create a poem in rhyme so instantly, Chandra Samsher was taken aback. Knowing that the poet was quite a genius, a title called 'Aansu Kavi'—one who can write poems instantly—was conferred to him. Since then he began to be recognized as Aansu Kavi.

After he was titled Aansu Kavi by His Majesty Chandra Samsher, Poet Dhungel also got a job at a customs office in the district headquarters. His rank was that of a *mukhiya* – a junior clerk. A magazine named *Gorkhali* used to be printed at the time. Dhungel wrote for it, and published such sorts of poems from which Nepal and its people would be benefited.

In the magazine *Chandrika*, his essays titled 'Mahendramalli' and 'Junkiri' had been published, while his poems were published in *Sundari* in 1993 BS. He wrote all genres: stories, plays, poems, essays and so on.

In the meantime, a case was filed against the book *Makaiko Kheti* written by Krishna Lal Adhikari. Krishna Lal Adhikari was sent to prison and Shambu Prasad was sacked accusing that he had helped him. Economic condition of his house was really weak. So a big adversity came upon him. Then, he went to Banaras of India looking for job.

Upon reaching Banaras, he managed to publish poems written by other poets along with his own. He maintained his family expenses from that.

While living in Banaras, he launched a weekly magazine named *Rajbhakti* in 1983 BS. Since there was no stable source of income, it was difficult for him to survive.

He again returned to Nepal. Then, he stayed with his parents-in-law.

Before long, he was bed-ridden with a disease. He had no money to buy medicine for two months. So, he remained in bed. Ultimately, when the ailment had gone beyond cure, he died in 1986 BS on the day of Bhadra Krishna Asthami, the eighth day of bright fortnight. He was forty years old at the time. Three years before he died, his wife Kamala had died.

Shambhu Prasad had a sound knowledge of Nepali, Sanskrit, English, Hindi, Bengali, Urdu and Newari languages. He had learned these languages at home. He could read and write in these languages. Some novels and plays written by him in Hindi have been published. He has translated some Hindi novels into Nepali.

Poet Dhungel wrote many books in Nepali, but all these books have not been published and nobody knows the whereabouts of their manuscripts. Of all the books he wrote, altogether 23 have been published. He also edited and translated 5 books.

Given below are the books he wrote and published:
1. Panchak Prapancha, 2. Gaph Sindhu (collection of poems), 3. Chandra Pratap Barnan, 4. Chandrabadani, 5. Dootsatak, 6. Shambhu Bhajan Mala, 7. Mahabharatka Bibhinna Parba (1975 – 1983), 8. Beshya Baran, 9. Pinasko Binas, 10. Barhamase, 11. Dhruba Charitra, 12. Maitalu Chhoriko Katha, 13. Aansukavi Shambhuka Kavyakriti, 14. Malati Madhav (play), 15. Ashok Sundari (play), 16. Hattimtaiko Katha, 17. Gulavkawali, 18. Tota-Maina, 19. Birsikka, 20. Sunkesra Raniko Katha, 21. Abola Maiya, 22. Akbar-Birbal Binod, 23. Singhasan Battisi.

Given below are the books he edited and translated:
1. Shakuntal, 2. Uttar Ram Charitra, 3. Ratnawali, 4. Priyadarshika, 5. Sabdasudha Nidhi.

It was in Sambhu Prasad's works that the genres of prose found the first truly committed writer. Poetry, like prose, was always his favorite form. He is considered to be the writer who gave the highest number of books in the history of literature in the medieval era. His poems are beautiful. Some samples of his beautiful verses are like this.

Jhukchhan brikchha sadaiba phoola phalale bhaari
    hunda maa ati
Jhukchhan sajjana pai maana manamaa sekhi narakhi
    rati.

Har bakhat harek kurama dhyana hos Nepalako
Jun mulukama jaaun hami mana hos Nepalako
Janma bhumi dekhi badta chhaina kyei sansarama
Chittale tasabir khichi samman hos Nepalako.

Hare! Karma sarai malai chhakaais
Sabai sokhaharoo dekhi tadha garais
Ma launnthe taas tin khap pahile
Purana luga aaja tainle bhirais.

Namaskar sada gardachhu karmalai
Ma kasto thiye aaja kasto banais
Ajhai prana yo jhundiyekai chha jiuma
Bipat Shambhule paunu samma pais.

[The first stanza tells that the tree lowers when it is full of fruits; similarly a gentleman bows without any inhibition, if he is laden with virtues. The second stanza wishes, one could care for Nepal at all times; he could sing for the dignity of Nepal wherever he reaches. No place in the world is more valuable than the place of one's birth. One should respect Nepal with all his heart. The last verses say: 'Oh, Karma! you deceived me very much, taking me far away from my cravings. I used to wear layers of clothes before; now, you have forced old, tattered clothes on me. O, I was different; you reduced me so much. Still

I have a life to live, though I have difficulties to a large extent.]

Poet Dhungel started writing from an age of of fifteen. Initially, he wrote poems with pseudonym 'Sukesi' and 'Lawanyamay'. He was five years younger than Poet Lekhanath Paudyal by age, but he died thirty-six years, in 1986 BS, earlier than Lekhanath. His life remained short. He did not get the favorable environment and facilities. Despite all of these, whatever he did for Nepali literature will keep him alive and we bow our heads with respect while remembering him.

After the death of a quite laborious and pleasant poet, the government has issued a postal stamp in his commemoration. Though he did not get any award and title besides 'Aansu Kavi,' he is familiar as an immortal genius of Nepal.

■

Poet Dharanidhar Koirala

Jaaga jaaga aab jaaga na jaaga,
Laaga unnatibise aba laag.
Ghora neend ab taa parityaaga,
Bho bhayo ati sutyou aba jaaga.
Deshbandhuharoo ho! utha jaaga.

[Awake ! Awake ! Awake ! Now, march towards prosperity. Give up your deep sleep; it is too bad that you have slept so much. Awake, my countrymen!]

The famous poet who wrote these beautiful lines in Nepali language was none other than Dharanidhar Koirala. He was born at Dumja village of Sindhuli District on 24th Magh 1949 BS. Though born in a backward and remote hilly region, he possessed a strong desire to earn education. Hence, he went to Banaras in India.

Studying diligently in Banaras, he passed his I.A. After this, he completed B.A. and B.T., and also took army training. In addition, he studied Sanskrit language.

A poet awakening people to work for the nation, Dharanidhar Koirala was diligent and promising. He had much affection for his country and language since his early days. During his stay in Banaras, a weekly newspaper *The Gorkhali* used to be published from there. He worked for that newspaper and got his patriotic poems published. After some time, the Ranas put a ban on the publication of the newspaper.

His numerous poems were also published in the monthly Nepali newspaper *Chandrika* which was published from Kharsang, India. He was already popular in Darjeeling because of those heart-touching poems he composed and got published. His thoughts, intelligence and wisdom had already impressed people there. Everyone likes a patriotic, intellectual, and honest person. People liked him very much and entreated him to settle down there; consequently, he became an inhabitant of Darjeeling.

Though he remained in a foreign land for a long time, Dharanidhar never forgot his country and mother tongue. With the poem "Jaaga Jaaga" that helped develop the country and awaken the people and the poem "Ab Ke Eshai Ladi Bhidikan Marne", he kept on awakening and convincing people to advance to strive for progress and prosperity.

Dharanidhar wrote many books, but only three of them are published. Those books are:
1. Naibedya, 2. Spandan, 3. Shreemad Bhagawatgita (translation).

He also has some other miscellaneous poems to his credit.

Whatever he wrote was written in accordance with the context. He contributed mainly to the popularizing of education and Nepali literature. His language was heart-touching and simple. He wrote poems that everyone could easily understand. Everyone likes his style. So, he has become a very popular poet.

Dharanidhar was indeed a devotee of literature. He spent all his life in the service of his country, language and society. He always thought of his motherland as greater than heaven. To uplift his motherland and to empower his race, he often summoned his countrymen thus:

Prananta hos tara dhyan rakhaun
Nepalako mana-gumana rakhaun.

[Let life end, but remember, you must always maintain the prestige and glory of Nepal.]

Dharanidhar made such requests to his countrymen right from his earliest poems. Recognizing his love for his country and language, affection and belief in countrymen, and his social work, Royal Nepal Academy honored him with Tribhuvan Puraskar for his long service to Nepali literature. He also became an honorary member of the Academy. He expired on 26th Magh 2036 BS in Kathmandu.

Dharanidhar was one among three people Suryabikram Gyawali, Dharanidhar Koirala, and Paras Mani Pradhan, renowned by the acronym 'Sudhapa', who contributed to the development of Nepali language and literature abroad, i.e. in Darjeeling.

■

Linguist Mahananda Sapkota

Basundhara swarga manushya
*   debata*
Sewa yinaiko parmartha marga
*   hun.*
Saparnaka lagi manushya purpuro
Jibro bisayera chalau pakhuro.

[The verses say that if the world is heaven, people are gods. Service to people is the most divine of all paths. In order to improve human intellect, one should stop talking, and commit to working.]

The name of the poet who wrote such insightful verses is Mahananda Sapkota. He was born on 30 Baisakh 1953 BS in the village called Dewanchhap of Ilam District, Mechi Zone. He was the son of an ordinary farmer Ram Chandra Sapkota.

There were no schools in his village at the time. So, in order to teach him, his father took him to Assam of India. At first, he attended a school in Assam and later passed his high school from Darjeeling. He had a good knowledge of Sanskrit too. He also studied astrology.

After clearing his high school, Sapkota returned to Nepal. There was Rana rule in Nepal at the time. Children of our country were not allowed education. People who were educated were very few; yet, most of them did not have jobs. The rich people used to suppress the downtrodden.

Sapkota saw such kinds of unscrupulous conducts in his society. He thought of doing something to bring justice to the innocent village folks. He thought that, first of all, man should become understanding or conscientious.

Political consciousness should be given to them in order to overthrow the Rana regime, which had been leading people towards unequal conducts.

With these resolution, he started writing poems, basically to teach people good behavior. He also felt that it was necessary to send children to school.

First of all, he went to Calcutta of India and helped to launch a political party collaborating with a leader named Subarna Samsher. After returning to Nepal from there, he opened schools in Dharan and Dankuta. After that, visiting door to door, he encouraged the parents to send their children to those schools. He himself taught the students enrolled there.

At the time, not only children, even the adults would not write and use language correctly. He did not like that. And then, he actively participated in serving Nepali language, and was soon recognized as a multi-lingual person. He wrote books to teach children speak and write correctly. With a thought that the society should develop a kind of positive attitude to throw deeply-rooted bad behaviors, he wrote poems.

Let's see an example of the poem Sapkota wrote:

Bajdachha pwanga gagari ritto; bhari ta bajdaina
Sajjan gyani kahilyai pani phutani gardaina.

Sayama das-panch dhani ganinu
Arule tinaka kariya baninu.
Bidhiko yadi yei chha bidhana bhane
Aba tyo bidhiko pani aayu pugyo.

[The first stanza says a gentleman never shows his hubris. A half-filled pitcher spills; a full one doesn't. The second verse claims that if a few people considered rich enslave others, and that is the rule of fate, fate has its days numbered.]

Thinking that only writing poems and books of grammar and language was not enough, he opened a literary institution called Nepali Bhasha Pracharak Sangh in Korfok of Ilam District. The books he wrote are 23 in number. Given below are his books.

Language and Grammar: 1. Janajibro, 2. Sarishabda, 3. Chanchun, 4. Kriyanwayi Byanjana, 5. Nepali Nirbachanko Rooprekha, 6. Dhwaniko Dhanda, 7. Nepali Dhatu Parichaya, 8. Nepali Shabda Parichaya, 9. Khas ra Khas Bhasha.

Collection of Essays: 1. Sapkota Nibandhawali, 2. Hamro Sahitya (part 1), 3. Hamro Sahitya (part 2), 4. Hamro Sahitya (part 3), 5. Hamro Sahitya (part 4), 6. Nepali Bhasha (collection of essays).

Articles: 1. Sukkhako Bato, 2. Nepal Kasto Hunuparchha?

Song: 1. Manlahari.

Collection of Poems: 1. Apungo, 2. Aannu, Aasha, Aansu, 3. Aante, 4. Bishal Nepal, 5. Hamro Nepal.

Sapkota had prepared a book named *Nalibelisahitko Nepali Shabdakosh*, but the book has not been published till now. He also edited the magazines *Nepal Pukar* and *Hamro Nepal*.

Sapkota was given Madan Puraskar in 2027 BS and Indra Rajya Laxmi Pragya Puraskar in 2031 BS, for the beautiful books in Nepali language and literature he wrote. He also was conferred the title 'Gorkha Dakshinbahu.' He was felicitated in Biratnagar in 2031 BS.

While still actively involved in the work of literature and society even in an old age, Mahananda Sapkota passed away on 1 Ashad 2035 BS in Biratnagar. He is known as a linguist, writer, poet and social worker to modern Nepali society.

■

Writer Jhapat Bahadur Rana

Udyogi khanchha aaphule
Arkalai khuwaunchha.
Alchhi aaphai dukha paai
Jahan bachchha ruwaunchha.

[The industrious ones feed themselves, and also feed others. Those who are lazy fall themselves into difficulty, and pull their family into hardship.]

Yo yesto chha bhani pura
Manisa nachinikana
Nahos kasaisanga pani
Byavahara kunai dina.

[Before we know a man well, it is not fair to pass judgment: he is like this, or like that.]

The name of the poet who wrote such beautiful poems is Jhapat Bahadur Rana. He is not only a poet, but also a story writer and an essayist. A child of the Rana family, he was born on 5 Kartik 1953 BS in Dhobichaur of Kathmandu. His father's name was Bhairav Bahadur Rana and his mother's name Yog Kumari. It is said that he had seen Lord Shankar in dream when he was four years old. He believed that the Lord blessed him with the power to die on will.

Jhapat Bahadur learned the alphabet from his mother at home. His mother taught him how to write as well. The book he read for the first time was *Gajendramoksha* by Motiram Bhatta. He did not attend at any Sanskrit or English medium school. He read many books at home. By the time his *bratabandha* was performed, he had finished reading many books of Nepali, Sanskrit, English, and Newari languages.

Jhapat Bahadur fell seriously ill four months after he got married. Even water would not pass through his throat, and he always required pillow support. No any medicine cured his illness. Sitting by his side, his mother would read "Mahamrityunjaya", the Vedic mantra believed to defeat death. All hopes abandoned, the doctors had suggested the family to take him to the ghat—cremation gound—to await death.

In such a state of health, a strange dream occurred to Jhapat Bahadur one day. In the dream, a man, who looked with one eye, came at his door. He caught the right wrist of him and said, "Let me see who the dying man is." Taking out a tiny thread from his wrist he added, "This man is *not* going to die!" And then, he disappeared.

Jhapat awoke. He became graceful. After that, he recovered gradually. Thereafter, such a serious disease never attacked him.

In Bhadra 1972 BS, Prime Minister Chandra Samsher appointment him a lieutenant in the army. In the same year, he went to India to take part in World War I. After the battle, he returned Nepal in Falgun, the same year.

Upon his return to Nepal, his contact grew with many writers like Kavi Shiromani Lekhnath Paudyal, poet Shambu Prasad Dungel, and poet Baijanath Sedain. He wrote poems, stories, essays, and diaries, but his composition were not published rightaway. With help from the poets he had been in contact, his first works were published in *Sharada* and *Gorkhapatra*. One of his poems goes like this:

Swadeshama rahi khanu pitho chha meetho.
Bideshi mithaai pani ho namitho.

[At home, even grit is of wonderful taste, while in the lands abroad, even sweets do not taste good.]

Risa ho sabaiko bairi, sara kaama bigarane
Tasartha garnu abhyasa risako bega rokane.

[Anger is a foe to all; it spoils everything. One should practice to control the passion of anger.]

While sending his stories and essays to *Sharada* and *Gorkhapatra*, he would send bundles and bundles of them. Editors would take a few out of them and publish. Because he wrote during long sessions of leisure, his compositions were many.

In Bhadra 1978 BS, he was appointed the Chief District Officer of Syangja District. After that, he held similar posts in Kaski, Jhapa and Morang. In 1988 BS, he was suspended from the post. Later on, he was reinstated to the job, and made the Chief District Officer of Doti.

In 1990 BS, he settled down in Baneshwar of Kathmandu, buying a house of his own. Again, he took part in the World War II. After the war was over, he returned to Nepal.

In 1994 BS, Jhapat's father died. Soon after, he became a magistrate at the apex court. In 2009 BS, he quit his job. Jhapat Bahadur was given Dirghasewapatta for his long service.

His mother passed away in the same year. Since 2014 BS, he started living at Bandipur of Siraha District. In leisure, he would busy himself weeding his farm, with a small hoe in hand. If anyone ridiculed him, he would not speak back; rather, he would express himself in a poem. Such a poet died on 14 Paush 2030 BS on the bank of Kamala River at Bandipur of Siraha.

Though only a few discrete poems were published in his life time, Jhapat Bahadur's compositions were posthumously published as a book, edited by different writers. His published works include the following:

Stories: 1 Saundarya, 2. Jhapatka Das Kathaharoo.

Poems: 1. Smritika Kehi Pristhaharoo, 2. Samjanaka Chhalharoo, 3. Bhanjhayangka Suseliharoo.

Essays: 1. Jhapat Nibandhawali, 2. Gahan Chintan.

Besides these, there are many uncollected works yet to be compiled. If these works are published, many books will be added to the archive of Nepali literature. The autobiography and diaries he wrote too are awaiting a publisher's notice.

After his death in 2037 BS, a literary committee named "Jhapat Prize Management Committee" has been formed. The Committee gives 'Jhapat Prize' to writers every year. Many books written on him have been published. Students at Tribhuvan University have written dissertations on him. In this way he has become immortal even after death.

■

Historian Surya Bikram Gyawali

Historian Surya Bikram Gyawali was born in Jestha, 1955 BS to Til Bikram Gyawali and Parbati Devi.

As he was born in Banaras, his study began there. The school he attended was Harishchandra High School. He began studying from grade three there. After completing his high school, he passed B.A. from Calcutta  University, and again passed B.T. from the same University in the first division. B.T. stands for Bachelors Degree in Teaching.

He used to read a lot of stories and articles since a very small age. Because of that habit a special interest in literature brewed up inside him. A feeling of writing and doing 'something' stimulated him. He began writing articles filled with nationality since a young age of sixteen or seventeen. With a thought to oversee history of Nepal, language and literature, he devoted his time to that effect, day and night. Researching about great personalities of history, he began writing a book himself. Likewise, he, with a great care, edited the *Ramayana* by Bhanubhakta, and got it published. He also organized a literary conference in Darjeeling. Before that, *Ramayana* had not been edited in such a beautiful way with that much of hard-work in Nepali. It was his one of the most important works.

Around 1980s, he entered Darjeeling as a teacher to teach Nepali language and worked at Darjeeling High School, becoming its principal after some time. He taught as well as served Nepali language and literature. From his initiation,

Birat Nepali Literature Conference was organized in Darjeeling and an institution called Nepali Literature Conference was established. With this institutional work, Nepali language began to spread even out of the mainland of Nepal.

From the collaboration of three linguists and litterateurs, a linguistic and literary movement was launched. The credit goes to Surya Bikram Gyawali, Dharanidhar Koirala and Paras Mani Pradhan. With the first two letters of their own names, they made a group called 'Sudhapa'. The first name in Sudhapa is that of Suryabikram Gyawali.

Gyawali came to Kathmandu in 2013 BS. Here, he began to work as the Director of Archeological Department. After forming Royal Nepal Academy—now Nepal Academy—he worked as its Member Secretary. Later, he even became its Chancellor.

His primary interest was to research on Nepali language, chronicle and culture. He has written many books. His main books are these:

1. Drabya Shah, 2. Ram Shah, 3. Prithivi Narayan Shah, 4. Bir Balabhadra, 5. Amar Singh Thapako Jeevani.

Along with these, *Nepalko Madhyakalin Itihas*, *Bhanubhaktako Ramayan* (edited) and *Katha Kusum* (edited) are works to his credit.

Besides these, he prepared many research articles, prefaces and historical documents.

Gyawali was awarded with Tribhuvan Puraskar in 2028 BS and Prithvi Pragya Puraskar in 2040 BS for his tireless service to Nepali language, literature and history. That time, he was the second person to claim Prithivi Puraskar. The prize was of one hundred thousand rupees. The prize was given to him respecting his entire literary personality and and his remarkable service in the development and prosperity of Nepali language and literature for a long time, and his invaluable contribution to heighten the pride of the nation. The prize is handed over only to those people who serve in the field of language, science and culture for a long time.

Gyawali's personality glittered as a historian, explorer and critic. He passed away on 16 Mangsir 2042 BS in Kathmandu.

■

Riddhi Bahadur Malla : A Patron of Literature

Riddhi Bahadur Malla has helped many Nepali writers gain popularity. He has translated many works of foreign language into Nepali. He published writings of many literary figures in his magazine. It used to be a matter of pride to get a writing published in any magazine those days.

Giving jobs at his publication, he encouraged many writers to write fine literature. His magazine *Sharada* was highly popular those days. It was the first literary magazine of Nepal to introduce different genres of modern literature to the general readers.

Malla's ancestral home was in Kathmandu Valley. But, his family lived in Banaras of India, mainly for job.

While his parents were in Banaras, Riddhi Bahadur was born on 24 Mangsir 1955 BS. His father's name was Bir Bahadur Malla and mother's name Nir Kumari. His father died when Riddhi was just five. Hence, he grew up in his mother's care.

After some time of his father's death, his mother took him to Kathmandu. They were extremely poor at the time. His brother's legs had been broken when he fell from the verandah of their house. He would always keep crying of extreme pain. His mother gave sweets to console him. Young Riddhi also wanted some of them, but couldn't ask for it.

So, one day Riddhi said to his mother, "Mom! If my legs too were broken by falling from the verandah, I would also get candies as Brother does, won't I?" His words filled his mother's eyes with tears, and she became speechless. He sensed she didn't have money to buy sweets for him. And then, wiping tears on his mother's eyes, he said, "Mom! Please do not cry. Now onward, I will never ask you to buy me anything. I know you don't have money."

All his life, he never did anything that would hurt the feelings of his mother.

Hriddhi learnt the alphabet from his mother at the age of six. Schools in Nepal had started teaching English by the time. Hence, he also began to learn English. His teachers Madan Dev and Lala taught him English.

He took admission at the Durbar High School in 1964 BS. He was twenty years old when he was studying in the tenth grade. At that time, students had to go to Kolkata to appear the high school passing examination. So, he also went to Kolkata with friends. He passed matriculation in 1976 BS from there. And then, he came back to Kathmandu.

Putting 'dosalla', a two-fold woolen shawl, upon his successful matriculation, he was given an elephant ride round Kathmandu Valley. That used to be the practice of felicitation those days. The practice discontinued after 1977 BS. Riddhi was probably the last graduate to move round on an elephant's back.

After he passed his high school, Riddhi couldn't continue his study further. He had to look after his family. He started working to manage everyday life. He got a job at the palace of Prime Minister Juddha Samsher's daughter's palace at Ramnagar. He had to toil hard from morning till evening. Hence, there was no question that he could continue his study.

After some time, he came to Kathmandu and began to work in Bag Durbar. He hadn't read many Nepali books while he was a student at Durbar High School. So, he thought of reading books of Nepali language. He also thought of writing and publishing the books in Nepali. With this thoughts, he started immersing in reading, and got completely absorbed.

In the meantime, he began writing works of his own, and encouraged other authors to write, too. He authored a novel and named it *Sharmishtha*. He got it published from Motihari of India in 1985 BS, when he had reached there. Thereafter, he translated many literary works of other languages into Nepali.

After he came to Kathmandu from India, he founded a printing press named Jor Ganesh Press. He printed court documents there. He also began printing books written by men of the palace.

Rudraraj Pandey was his close colleague. After he became the Principal of Tri-Chandra College, he decided to publish a literary magazine from Nepal. Till then, no literary magazine had ever been published from Nepal. In fact, the Ranas didn't let anyone publish a magazine.

Decided on doing this, they placed the request with Juddha Samsher the Prime Minister: "Your Majesty, please let us release a monthly literary magazine."

Juddha Samsher agreed. That was an approval. Riddhi Bahadur printed the issue of the literary magazine named *Sharada*, destined to become one of the most historic magazines in the history of Nepali literature. The first volume of *Sharada* appeared on 1 Magh 1991 BS. The magazine was printed at Riddhi's Jor Ganesh press.

Although he himself published *Sharada*, Riddhi hired other people to edit it. Siddhi Charan Shrestha, Bhawani Bhikshu, Gopal Prasad Rimal, and Govida Bahadur Malla 'Gothale' edited the magazine. An editor, as you know, edits, revises, cuts unnecessary items, grants permission to publish, and makes corrections in the works that are to be published.

Writings of the famous writers of that age, including Lekhnath Paudyal, Laxmi Prasad Devkota, Bal Krishna

Sama, Siddhi Charan Shrestha, Madav Prasad Ghimire, Bishweshwar Prasad Koirala, Gopal Prasad Rimal, Rudra Raj Pandey, Prem Raj Sharma, Bhawani Bhikshu, Shyam Das Vaishnab, and many others were published in *Sharada*. Considered later to be the heavyweights of Nepali literature, all these writers were initially given a base by *Sharada*. If the magazine was not there, Nepali literature would not have been so rich. Though *Sharada* was the single magazine of Nepal, it was not the best-selling. Therefore, Riddhi had to bear gradual loss. Eventually, he abandoned the publication.

Though *Sharada* was closed, Riddhi's desire to publish a magazine was intact in him. Soon he started a daily paper named *Aawaj*. That was the first daily paper of Nepal in private sector. The first issue of it was published on 7 Falgun 2007 BS. Siddhi Charan Shrestha was the editor and Riddhi Bahadur the publisher. After some time, *Aawaj* too was closed. Although it was closed, Riddhi's heart never closed, and his readiness to serve Nepali literature never subsided.

His published works are these:

Novel: 1. Sharmishta.

Translated Novels: 1. Aankhako Kashingar, 2. Dunga Paltiyo, 3. Shes Prashna, 4. Charitraheen, 5. Gora, 6. Nyatridyamko Kumbhe.

He translated many other books too. But, these translations have not been published. His books, which are yet to be published are: 1. Shah Jahan, 2. Guru-Sishya Samvad, 3. Shakuntal, 4. Geeta and, 5. Yuddha ra Shanti.

Besides these, many stories, essays and criticisms he wrote have not been published. He has written an autobiography too. It is yet to be published.

Among his sons, Govinda Bahadur Malla 'Gothale' and Bijaya Malla became famous literary figures. They continued his line of work.

Towards the end of his life, Riddhi began to write an autobiography. Moreover, he had a plan to translate many foreign books into Nepali. But slowly, he lost his eyesight. That's why, doctors advised him not to involve in such works. And then, he couldn't write. He often regretted that he couldn't serve literature much. After some time, he died on 5 Baishakh 2025 BS.

Riddhi Bahadur didn't get any awards as long as he was alive. A postal stamp was issued in his name in 2054 BS. However, nobody can forget the magnanimity he showed for the promotion of Nepali literature. He is a great jewel of Nepal.

■

Nepali Linguist Paras Mani Pradhan

Paras Mani Pradhan was born in Magh, 1955 BS in Kalimpong of Darjeeling, Bengal Province of India in 1955 BS.

A long time ago, his father had migrated to the plains from high eastern hills of Okhaldunga District of Nepal for business. Gradually, his father, changing the location, settled at a place called Sindubung. At that time, there were five members in his family: father, mother, Paras Mani and two brothers.

After he reached five, his father admitted him to a school. Since the school was far from their home and the way was quite difficult, his father transferred him to another school. He kept on studying at home.

After some time, enrolling at Scottish Universities Mission School, he continued his education there. At the time, there was a tradition to give prize to those students, who could tell their lessons by heart. The ones who could not manage it, would be punished.

One day, Paras Mani could not read his assignment in front of the teacher. His ears were boxed. Blood oozed out of the ears. The earring worn in one of them fell out of it. Seeing the condition of the son, his parents— very much affectionate—withdrew him from the school.

Then, for some time, he helped parents in their household works. His task at home was to graze cattle and goats. He had a desire to study from within his heart, though. As the saying goes, 'Moustache cannot stop one from eating,' he continued his study freely. After some time, he and his brother got an opportunity to go to Darjeeling for study. There, following extremely hard work, he passed his matriculation in the first division. After that, he passed I.A. and B.A. from private study.

Until he had cleared his high school, his name was 'Prasaman.' He began writing in Nepali language. Initially, he got his poems and articles published in a monthly Nepali magazine called *Chandra* printed from Kashi. He began to publicize Nepali language and literature by writing poems, articles and stories in the weekly Nepali magazine named *Gorkhali* printed also from Kashi.

At the same time, he taught at Darjeeling High School. However, he left the job after some time. As a free man, he began to involve in writing and serving Nepali language and literature.

He launched a Nepali magazine called *Chandrika*. He relentlessly moved forward to serve Nepali language and literature as an editor, writer and publisher, though quite away from home. With this work, his genius came out. After that, Nepali language spread away from homeland. Nepali language and literature developed pretty much.

The main books, he wrote are as follows:

1. Nepali Dictionary, 2. Bhasha Prabesh, 3. English Nepali Dictionary, 4. Nepali English Dictionary, 5. Nepali Bengali Dictionary, 6. Tipantapan Kavita Sangraha, 7. Panch Paurakhi Purushharooko Jeevani.

Along with these, he has written many works for children, enriching the store of Nepali language and literature.

Royal Nepal Academy awarded Paras Mani with Tribhuvan Puraskar in 2025 BS, for he continually served Nepali language and literature even while living abroad. Tribhuvan University honored him with honorary Ph.D. in 2030 BS for his service to Nepali language and literature.

Since his ancestral home was in Patna, he searched and found it out and expressed his pleasure reaching there. He certainly paid due respect to Nepali language and literature, even by also reaching back to the house where his ancestors lived. He shared his experience with other litterateurs: "It was like going on a pilgrimage."

Even today, Paras Mani is famous as a versatile, hardworking author, an expert linguist and a renowned personality, not only within homeland but also outside in the foreign lands. The name of Surya Bikram Gyawali, Dharanidhar Koirala and Paras Mani Pradhan—that is 'Sudhapa'—is taken with high honor in Darjeeling and in Nepal. Of them, he is one.

He died on 20 Magh 2040 BS.

■

Story Writer Guru Prasad Mainali

One doesn't have to write many stories to become a famous story writer. Just a few stories, which are liked and understood by everyone, are sufficient to make someone renowned. We can acquire the same message from Guru Prasad Mainali.

The ancestral home of Guru Prasad Mainali lies in Kanpur Village of Kavrepalanchok District. His father Kashinath Mainali was a government employee. In course of his service, his father went to the district headquarters of Dhankuta where *gainda-goswara*—district administrative offices and courts—were located. He worked in one of these offices.

Guru Prasad was born while his father was there in Dhankuta in 1957 BS on sukla chaturdasi of Bhadra, the fourth day of bright lunar fortnight in the month of Bhadra.

Mainali, the son of Kashinath and Rupa Devi was sharp-minded and quite intelligent from a very young age. He was indeed destined to be a genius. He would put forth unusual type of logic in any reasoning. On hearing his arguments, even grown up people would be taken aback. He was skillful in giving multiple meanings and explanations even to a small point. So, people predicted what sort of man he would become on growing up.

Guru Prasad couldn't acquire high education. He didn't live in one place permanently because he had to go with his father as his father moved from one place to other as a jobholder. He learnt the alphabet at home. As he grew, he was taught scriputures like *Laghukaumudi, Amarkosh, Rudri, Durgasaptasati* and so on.

Then he attended a *shresta* school—a middle school opened especially for bureaucratic training. There were not many schools at that time in Nepal. Among the few that existed, Durbar High School was assumed to be the best, but it was in Kathmandu. Some other schools were scattered in eastern Nepal, western Nepal and Tarai. There were only ordinary schools in other places.

After he completed his study at the *shresta* school, Guru Prasad took a job in judicial service. He started the job from the rank of a nausinda—a lower grade official in clerical profession. His salary was eleven rupees per month. Later, he became a bichari— clerk in a court, and dittha— an official ranked below a non-gazette officer, and tahsildar—a collector of revenues and taxes. And then, he became a magistrate. It was not a joke to become a magistrate, because he had not aquired high education and above that, he was from an ordinary family. As he became a magistrate in the time of the Rana regime, he knew internal realities of the Ranas.

Guru Prasad presided over the preceedings of many domestic cases after he became a magistrate. As he scritunized such cases time and again, he knew what sort of situation was there in the village. He traveled from village to village of Nepal. He saw poor people in the villages and also knew why people would become poor. He saw the relationship of husband and wife, of brothers and friends, of neighbours and of many more. Many events were quite serious and heart-rending. As he knew such heart-rending cases, he got an inspiration to write stories based on them.

He began to feel how beautiful it would be to write stories about the events. Thereafter, thinking with great care, he began writing stories. With great care and thought, he wrote stories on the incidents he had seen, in a language understandable to everyone. Besides, he visited many places of Nepal and India. So he knew even about minor incidents that took place in the villages. Even such minor incidents touched his heart painfully. So, he reflected all these experiences in the stories he wrote. He also wrote stories about the struggle and suffering of the Nepali people who went to work in India.

The story he wrote for the first time was "Naso." It was published in *Sharada*, a literary magazine, in 1992 BS. The story earned pretty much popularity. He was inspired and encouraged from every nook and corner. He knew that such type of stories would bring him more popularity. Before that, there was no common practice to write stories on the basis of a simple event of ordinary families.

Upon getting the story "Naso" published, a new practice developed in story writing. Guru Prasad became the man to pioneer the new practice. And then, stories written by others also imitated his style. He wrote other stories, for he had received much appreciation from the story "Naso." In quick succession, he got the stories published one after another : "Paralko Aago," "Bida," and "Sahid." His stories titled "Chhimeki," and "Kartavya" grabbed high recognition. As a whole, all his stories were considered quite exceptional. He became the example of the thinking that writing only a few but excellent stories can earn a writer an undying popularity.

Though Guru Prasad wrote stories and got published in different magazines, he did not publish a book in his life time. Later in 2020 BS, a prolific critic Taranath Sharma collected Guru Prasad's stories and got them published in a collection named *Naso*. He became the editor himself. On getting the stories of Guru Prasad in a book form, the readers of Nepali literature became extemely happy.

Guru Prasad lived in Kathmandu after he quit his job. He passed away on 25 Jestha 2028 BS in Kathmandu itself. Upon his death, we lost a legendary story writer of Nepal forever.

Guru Prasad had published some pieces in the genre of comedy and essays too. But these writings have not been published as a book yet. He was not conferred any prizes, honors, and titles while he was alive. After a long time after his death, "Mainali Katha Puraskar" has been established in his name by a literary association named Sahityik Patrakar Sangh—the association of the literary journalists.

■

Novelist and Educationist
Rudra Raj Pandey

Roopamati is the first notable social novel of Nepal. This novel is quite renowned. The writer of this novel is Rudra Raj Pandey. He was also a historian and educationist.

Rudra Raj was born on 26th Falgun 1975 BS at Peuta Tole of Kathmandu. Padma Raj Pandey was his father and Tika Laxmi his mother. His father and maternal uncle were prudent scholars of Sanskrit. Rudra Raj had learned Sanskrit stanzas by heart from his maternal uncle at home. As he grew up, he was enrolled at Ranipokhari Sanskrit School. Later, he wanted to study English. And then, he got himself enrolled in grade 3 at Durbar High School for English education.

Although classes were conducted in Kathmnadu, the final examination was taken by Calcutta University of India. Rudra Raj Pandey too went to Calcutta for his examination and passed the same in the first division at the age of eighteen. Thereafter, he received government scholarship and passed I.A., B.A., and M.A. in history from Allahabad, India.

Just another day after passing out his master's degree examination, Pandey got an appointment as a lecturer at Tri-Chandra College and as Principal at Durbar High School of Kathmandu in 1981 BS. After teaching at both these institutions for some time, he went to India and arranged the process to allow Nepali students to take their examination in Nepal itself. India agreed to recognize the examination taken in Nepal as its equivalent. This way, he managed to administer School Leaving Certificate Examination for Nepali students from Nepal.

Pandey was appointed Principal of Tri-Chandra College in 1995 BS. He worked at this capacity till 2008 BS. During his tenure, he procured permissions to teach biology, botany, geography, and political science at intermediate level and began running classes for B.Sc. as well. He organized many debates and writing competitions at the College. Only because of his efforts, Patna University of India gave recognition to Nepali as a major subject. His time onwards, examination of Sanskrit also started taking place in Kathmandu.

During the tenure of Rana Prime Minister Padma Samsher, Rudra Raj Pandey worked pretty hard to draft the laws of Nepal in 2004 BS. After the political change of 2007 BS, he became the Deputy Secretary at the Ministry of Education. After some time, he became the Election Commissioner, the chief executive of the Election Commission. The Commission held elections in Nepal for the first time. He left government service in 2017 BS. But again, King Mahendra appointed him the Vice-Chancellor of Tribhuvan University in 2021 BS. After he became the Vice-Chancellor, Tribhuvan University progressed very much.

Pandey was interested in literature since childhood. He often met writers at the office of the Pashupati Publication at Fasikeb in Kathmandu. They would gather at Machhindra Bahal, too. He got familiar with Lekhnath Paudyal, Shambu Prasad Dungel, and Krishna Lal Adhikari at the same place. Then, he became very much active in the field of literature. His poems were published in Nepali magazines named *Chandra* and *Chandrika* published from India as he was studying at a university there. His poems were also published in a magazine named *Suktisindhu* published from Nepal. He established friendship with the litterateurs Sumitranandan Panta and Parasu Ram Chatuberdi as he was staying in India. Because of his keen interest in Nepali language and literature, he made an effort to open 'Nepali Language Publication Committee.' After the S.L.C. exams started taking place in Nepal itself, Nepali books were needed. Hence, a 'Nepali Language Translation Council' was formed as per his suggestion. He incredibly contributed to publish *Sharada*, the literary magazine. And Riddhi Bahadur Malla was selected its editor.

Pandey published a novel named *Roopamati* in 1991 BS. A simple domestic story of Nepali society, the novel had became a very important publication. The book is popular even today. The novel has been translated into English and Urdu as well. Upon releasing *Roopamati* Pandey published the novels *Chappakaji, Prayaschita* and *Prem.* He also published a biographical book *Navaratna*, saying that it should inspire the reader love the country.

Writing a play to feel glory for the nation in childhood, he published two books of play, *Hamro Gaurav* and *Hamro Nepal.* Translating a story "Ishpanitikatha," he published it to give moral lessons to children. There were no books of history; so, he wrote histories of India and Britain and he got them published. He also wrote Nepal *Aajad Sangh Urph Sande Sangh,* a book of satire and comedy.

Pandey contributed enormously to Nepali language and literature. He received the title 'Gorkha Dakshinbahu,' in 1989 BS, 'Sardar' in 2002 BS and 'Trishaktipatta' in 2004 BS. He also got the medals on Silver Jubilee of His Majesty Tribhuvan's coronation, and later a medal on the coronation of His Majesty King Mahendra' and still later, a medal on the coronation of His Majesty King Birendra.

Pandey had deep faith in religion. He used to visit famous yogis and hermits and ascetics of Nepal. He would listen to them. He donated some amount of money to a society named 'Gaunsewa Kosh' for social works. He had given five acre of land of his own in Bara district for the provision of ascetics, pious people. He managed to offer 'Padma Raj Subarna Padak' to the one who passed S.L.C in the first division and Tikalaxmi Subarna Padak to a girl student who passed B. Sc. in the first division. He also deposited some money to provide Lilawallav Pant Suvarna Padak to those students who held first division in acharya examination – an examination in Sanskrit equal to master's. He opened a 'Fund of Scholarship' to provide scholarship to the disabled and brilliant students.

Books he wrote are these:

Novel: 1. Roopmati, 2. Chappakaji, 3. Prayaschit, 4. Prem 5. Herpher.

Collection of Stories: 1. Nabaratna.

One Act Play: 1. Hamro Gaurav, 2. Hamro Nepal.

Translation: 1. Ishap Neetikatha.

Satire and Comedy: 1. Nepal Aajad Sangh Urph Sande Sangh.

Culture and Religion: 1. Santa Darshan (part one), 2. Santa Darshan (part two).

History: 1. Bharatko Samchhipta Itihas (part one), 2. Bharatko Samchhipta Itihas (part two), 3. Englandko Itihas.

Rudra Raj Pandey died on 23 Chaitra 2043 BS. Upon his death, many meetings of reverential offerings were organized in his commemoration. In 2044 BS, a society named 'Rudra Raj Sahitya Sewa Samiti' was founded in his name. The society has been distributing Rudra Raj Puraskar every year since 2049 BS. Every year on the 26th of Falgun, Rudra Raj's birth anniversary is celebrated. In his memorial, books by other writers have been published. A postal ticket with his image has been issued by the postal department. Different magazines published volumes in his name.

His death caused an irreparable damage to Nepali literature. An influential literary figure like him is remembered for ever.

■

Pundit Sambabhakta Sharma Subedi

Jagga jodchhan dhanile har taraha
gari
Ha basai dukhi janchhan
Kheti garchhan najani maljal tarika
Ghatna go bali jhan-jhan.
Yesto chala hunale jamin rukhina
gai
Bhaisakyo kitana
Badhou jagga bhayeko kina yesari
hare
Dukha khepchhan kisana.

[Rich people always want to add land more and more but it goes worthless. They undertake farming without any idea of fertilizers and irrigation. The production, obviously, decreases. Because of such manner, land goes barren. Let's divide the land we have. Why do peasants face trouble like this?]

Such a beautiful poem was written by Sambabhakta Sharma Subedi. He was a proficient scholar, educationalist and poet of Nepal. He is called 'Samba Guru' also. 'Murari' and 'Madhudhara' are his nicknames. He is the brother-in-law of Krishna Lal Adhikari, Nepal's first literary martyr.

Subedi was born on the last day of Baishak in 1958 BS at Dumrikharkha Village of Ramechhap District. His father's name was Naranath Subedi and his mother's name Manorama Devi. Some of his family members despised him, calling by the derogatory name *'Pakhe'*—uncivilized— because they used to live in Kathmandu. Because of that insult, he resolved and started thinking how he could become popular, and more famous than others.

He forced his father to teach him the alphabet. His father too taught him how to write with a wooden cleft, putting dust on a board. Later, from the bark of mango, he made ink by cooking it, and started writing on sal leaves. He read and wrote a lot, even if he was a buffalo-herd. He was very laborious.

His *bratabandha*—initiation rite—was performed in 1966 BS. At that time, there was only one book—the *Ramayana*—at his home. He read the very book. Borrowing books from his relatives, he longed to read, but no one gave him. This generated in him an urge to study and procure for himself a number of books and digest them. His sister gave him a book named *Bibahalila*. After reading the book, he started reciting *siloks*—the couplets—on wedding ceremonies in the village. Then people started calling 'siloke keto'—the boy who recited *siloks*. Since then, he got a kind of taste of poetry and he started writing poems. He recited all the eighteen *Puranas*—great books of ancient Hindu mythology—sitting on the same spot. He was an erudite guy at his own time and his identity was also established as a *pauranik*—a pundit of mythologies, well-versed in Sanskrit.

Sambabhakta came to Kathmandu in Falgun, 1971 BS. Admitted at Tindhara School, he started his study in Falgun 1972 BS. After two years, he passed *prathama* – the primary level examination in Sanskrit. In the same year, he got married.

He got himself engaged in literary talk with his brother-in-law Krishna Lal and spontaneous poet Shambu Prasad Dhungel. Krishna Lal was the one who was later imprisoned by the Ranas for writing *Makaiko Kheti*, a satirical work targeted at the Ranas. Sambabhakta too was an associate in writing the book. But he was spared the sentence because they had no proof of his involvement.

He continued his study and passed *madhayama*— intermediate level examination. He went to Banaras of India to continue his study further. But because of political upheaval there, his study could not go ahead. He then returned home in the hills of Ramechhap.

After Sambabhakta reached Ramechhap, he began teaching at a language school. In 1980 B.S, his father died. And then he had hard time in supporting his family. He was transferred to Kathjhor first and later to Dolaka. He came to Kathmandu leaving the job in 1985 BS. Babu Ram Acharya, the eminent historian, helped him become a teacher again at Ramechhap. He then returned to Ramechhap.

In this way, he served as a government employee for twenty-three years, but he was not entitled for any pension at the time of his retirement. Later he suffered from tuberculosis. The death of his wife and children added to his shock and misery. However, he didn't lose heart; he kept working as usual with full commitment.

Subedi's compositions used to appear in *Gorkhapatra* even during the time of his stay in Ramechhap. Those poems were rewarded at times. He used to write problem-solving kinds of poems under the pseudonym 'Madhudhara.' He has written many poems. Here is a sample of what he wrote:

Hira, moti, pannajadit pinjada swachha basan
Subarnaiko sikri jhalala bidhujhain ramya sadan.
Phika parne sara kacha-kacha paradhin mahal
Sugako drishtima naraksari jhalkanchha sakala.

[Eventhough the cage is made of diamond, pearl and emerald, it is like a golden cage. Though it looks wonderful to the world, it is but a hell to the parrot that is inside.]

Subedi came back to Kathmandu in Paush, 2003 BS. At that time, he served the Ranas for some time, but could not get anything in return. Bhimbhakta Singh Basnet and Pundit Somnath Ghimire 'Vyas' had helped him at the time.

From 2014 BS to 2017 BS, he taught at Sanjeevani High School at Dhulikhel. After that, he began to read and write at home. While staying at Dhulikhel, he had written a short epic named *Satyabrata*. That book was published in 2022 BS. Many of his poems in discrete forms have been published in *Gorkhapatra*.

Inspired by comedian Basudev Luitel, Sambabhakta wrote an autobiography entitled *Sambabhakta Sharma Subedi* in 2032 BS. It was published in the same year. His published books are as follows: 1. Satyabrata (short epic), 2. Sambabhakta Sharma Subedi (autobiography), 3. Murari (eulogy).

His unpublished works are also many. But these works are within the access of his family alone. If his entire works are published, it will be a great contribution to Nepali literature. It will also heighten the status and fame of Sambabhakta's family and relatives.

Sambabhakta died on 27 Magh 2038 BS. After his death, many researches have been undertaken studies on his life and work. His contribution, therefore, can never be forgotten.

■

Madhav Prasad Devkota:
A Poetic Genius

*Biratale kamayeko aaphna yasha
    jaha phuli
Raheka nitya dekhinchhan bhayera
    hiunka chuli
Jhalkeka baala rabika parda kirana
    chanchal
Khulne himalako dekhchhaun jaha
    swarnima jhalmala
Isara gardachhan chilla halleka
    patale vana
'Talaka deshma shanti chhaina-
    chhaina' bhanikan
Bujhi yo bata thanera 'salkera shantima tala'
Pahad choddachhan hassi gari chhaharako chhal.*

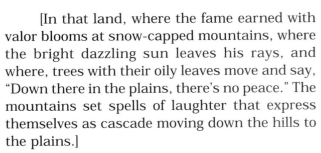

[In that land, where the fame earned with valor blooms at snow-capped mountains, where the bright dazzling sun leaves his rays, and where, trees with their oily leaves move and say, "Down there in the plains, there's no peace." The mountains set spells of laughter that express themselves as cascade moving down the hills to the plains.]

The above poem was written by Madhav Prasad Devkota. He is a great poet of Nepal. He has written poems and epics in Nepali and Sanskrit languages. He has also translated a few Sanskrit books into Nepali. Also an expert of Nepali language and grammar, he is a bright literary star of Nepal, who served our literature all his life.

Madhav Prasad Devkota was born on the last day of the dark fortnight on 3 Mangsir 1958 BS at Bhagawatitole,

Tansen of Palpa District. His father's name was Pushkar Nath Devkota and mother's name Narmada Devi. He learnt the alphabet from his own father at home.

Madhav's father was a scholar of Sanskrit. So, young Madhav also read Sanskrit before anything. He later came to Kathmandu from Palpa and studied up to intermediate at Rani Pokhari Sanskrit School. After that, he went to Banaras of India to study futher. From there in 1981 BS, he passed madhyama—intermediate degree—in the first division. And then, he abandoned his regular study and started teaching at the language school of Palpa in 1984 BS. He taught there for thirteen years, i.e. up to 2000 BS. Again, he went to Banaras to study further. In 2003 BS, he earned his bachelor's degree in the first division in religious studies. He then returned home and in 2004 BS, began teaching at Padma Public High School of Tansen as its headmaster. In 2011 BS, he became a part time teacher at the same school. He took retirement from there to continue his study, until he earned a postgraduate degree in Aryan Philosophy. Then, he became a lecturer at Tribhuvan College of Tansen. He became its Campus Chief for sometime. He taught there till Ashad, 2030 BS.

Magazines published in Sanskrit language from Banaras inspired him to write in Sanskrit. At the age of eighteen i.e. in 1978 BS, he started writing. But his compositions began to get published only in 1981 BS. In the same year, *Gorkhapatra* published his "Chandraki Chandrikale" a poem. This is his first published poem.

After that, Madhav continually engaged himself in the task of writing and publishing. After his essays began to appear in *Gorkhapatra* and his poems in *Sarbahitaisi* published from Banaras, his fame gradually rose and spread. Though he had begun writing in Sanskrit, he turned to Nepali in response to the call of time. So, his published works are both in Nepali and Sanskrit languages.

Although he wrote many works, his published works are as follows:

In Sanskrit: 1.Bharat Baibhavam, 2. Jeevan Danam, 3. Urmimala.

In Nepali: 1. Hussu Pathik, 2. Ruru Gaurav.

Collection of Poems: 1. Phoolbari, 2. Taranga.

Collection of Essays: 1. Lekhmala.

Grammar: 1. Kriya Chakra, 2. Nepali Bal Sanskrit Vyakaran, 3. Nepali Sanskrit Vyakaran (part 1 to 6).

Translation: 1. Ishadi Nau Upanishad,

2. Brihadaranyak Upanishad, 3. Chhandogya Upanishad.

Madhav Prasad Devkota has written other works, too. *Vidwanmoda Tarangini* translated by him from Sanskrit has not been published yet. *Kavita Kautukam*, a collection of poems written in Sanskrit is still an unpublished work. If we look for his works, still many of them can be found, waiting for someone to compile and publish.

In recognition of his knowledge and literary contribution, Madhav Prasad Devkota was honored by many organizations both from the governmental and non-governmental sectors. He was honored with the title 'Bidwatmani'—a gem of knowledge—by Kashi Academic Council of India in 2011 BS. Bharat Dharma Mandal conferred him with the title of 'Vidyabhushan.' Office of the Sanskrit Literature of Ayodhya, India awarded him the title 'Kaviratnam' — the poetic jewel— in 2014 BS. He also received the title 'Mahendra Vidyabhushan' from His Majesty King Mahendra in 2020 BS, and received the title 'Gorkha Dakshinbahu' from His Majesty King Birendra in 2030 BS.

On 6 Baishak 2036 BS, he was felicitated before a large gathering at Tundikhel, attended by litterateurs, journalists, artists, intellectuals, teachers, professors, industrialists and entrepreneurs of Palpa. He was given a ride through the municipality on a carriage. In the same year, he was awarded with 'Mahendra Pragya Puraskar.'

Madhav Prasad Devkota died on 10 Chaitra 2039 BS in Manikarnika of Banaras. At his death, Nepal lost a distinguished litterateur. He shall always be missed.

■

Pushkar Samsher: A Gifted Linguist

If the famous stories of Nepali literature are to be listed, the story 'Paribandha' figures among the few highest rated ones. The story is quite beautiful. How innocent people are trapped in the whirlwind of doubt has been shown in the story. The story was written by Puskar Samsher Rana.

Rana was born on 18 Paush 1958 BS in Gyaneshowar of Kathmandu. He was born in Rana family. His father's name was Samar Samsher and his mother's name Kriti Rajya Laxmi Devi. Rana was the first son of his parents. Bal Krishna Sama, his younger brother, is also a great litterateur of Nepal. He is well-known in the field of poetry and drama.

Til Madav Devkota, the father of the great poet Laxmi Prasad Devkota, taught him lessons in his childhood. He was keenly interested in studying. Since childhood, he would argue logically as he talked to people. They often performed dance at his house and at times, even staged plays. But he took interest in studying than in singing, dancing or performing. That's why, people called him 'bookish' in childhood.

Pushkar was a boy of good virtue since the time of childhood because he respected people senior to him, and loved his juniors. He never dominated and oppressed the people who worked at his home.

He had a habit of reading any kind of books with a great attention. He could not take his I.A. exams, because he fell ill at the time of examination.

He served the Royal NepaliArmy for some time. He had been upgraded up to the rank of Captain and Major in the Army. Since he was very much interested in reading and writing, he left the job in the Army soon.

He has greatly contributed to Nepali language and literature. He wrote and translated books of English into Nepali. Among the books he wrote are three course books and a book of grammar. Two books translated from English have been published. A collection of stories named *Pushkar Samsherka Katha* has also been published. A recently published collection of memoir about him helps remember the service he had done.

Given here are his published books:

On different subjects: 1. English-Nepali Dictionary (first part), 2. English-Nepali Dictionary (second part), 3. Nepali Proverbs, Maxims, Phrases, and Sayings.

Grammar: 1. Nepali Sajilo Vyakaran.

Translation: 1. She, 2. Othello.

Stories: 1. Puskar Samsherka Katha.

Among the stories he wrote, three stories titled 'Paribandha' 'Logne and 'Swarthatyag' are the most popular ones in Nepali literature. He is the one who, in spite of writing a few stories, is much talked about. A novel he wrote named *Sashubudhi* has not been published yet. Many other books of him might be still existent.

Pushkar Samsher became the Chairman of Nepali Language Translation Council in 1995 BS and then he became first a member and then the Chairman of Nepali Bhasha Prakashini Samiti. He was also a professor of Nepali at Tri-Chandra College.

This literateur was also a faculty of English. He had found errors even in the famous English dictionaries prepared by English scholars. So, he was appreciated very much in Britain. The Englishmen did not, before that, know that a Nepali speaking person could be a scholar in English too.

He once went to London, the capital of Britain. He worked as a Nepali subject assistant teacher for T. W. Clark in 2009 BS, and at the School of Oriental and African Studies in 2011 BS. He popularized Nepali literature and language as far as he could.

Pushkar fell sick and remained unhealthy for a long time. Towards the end of his life, his hands and legs were paralyzed. He passed away on 10 Baisakh 2018 BS in Janakpur.

His contribution to Nepali language, literature and grammar is considerably immense. He is a highly valued literary figure of Nepali society.

■

Playwright Bal Krishna Sama

Bal Krishna Sama was born on 24 Magh 1959 BS in Gyaneshwar of Kathmandu. His father's name was Samar Samsher Janga Bahadur Rana and his mother's Kriti Rajya Laxmi Devi.

Sama's father had two sons: Pushkar Samsher and Bal Krishna Sama. Both the brothers have become immortal in the history of Nepali literature.

Scholars can predict the future of a child : what sort of a man he will become as he grows. It's like saying, morning shows the day. These two brothers had shown their genius in their young ages.

After he reached five in 1964 BS, Sama was taught the alphabet, starting on the day of Shree Panchami, the day when we mark Sarasawati Puja. The one who taught him letters was Til Madav Devkota, father of Laxmi Prasad Devkota, the great poet.

A lot of singing and dancing used to take place at Sama's house. At times, drama would be performed too. Sama would be greatly pleased, seeing the stage curtains decorated with colorful paintings. He enjoyed watching waltz. He had a great interest in acting since his early age. Because of the very amusing environment at home, he became a famous playwright, poet, philosopher, and artist. He made Nepali literature rich and thus heightened the prestige of Nepal.

He started writing poems when he was very young. His poem "Ishwar," the one he wrote at the age of ten, had been published in *Sharada*. At the age of 15 or 16, he began writing beautiful works.

One day, *Buddhi Binod*, a book of poems fell into his hand. It was written by Kavi Shiromani Lekhanath Paudyal. Reading that book, he was encouraged to write poems. Sama, who wanted to become a poet himself was blessed by Saraswati, the goddess of knowledge, in his dream one night. She asked him, "What blessings do you want?"

He cried out, "I want to be a poet, Mother."

"All right, your wish is granted!" Saraswati blessed him. That dream came true. He became renowned as a great poet. He was rich with real genius because he could write dramas in verses. Many a stanza of his poems in dramas have become extemely popular. For example:

Deshabhakti ta mardaina chutthai desh vaye pani
Patibhakti ta mardaina papi pati vaye pani.

Sahu sahu sahu babu! Sahanai nasakepani
Narayana yahi naam barambar liyi rahu.

Gyan mardachha hansera roi bigyan mardachha.

> [The first two lines say, "Patriotism never dies, even if it's a mean country; a woman's devotion to her husband remains, no matter how wicked man he is." The second couplet means, "Tolerate, dear, though it is difficult. Take the name of Narayan repeatedly, and tolerate." The last one says, "Knowledge dies with a smile, while science dies with tears."]

A student of Durbar High School—now Bhanu Secondary School—Sama passed his matriculation from Calcutta. After that, while studying at Tri-Chandra College, he entered the army service against his own will. He was upgraded to the rank of Major General. Then, he engaged himself in teaching Nepali at Durbar High School and Tri-

Chandra College in 1987 BS. He worked as the Chairman of Nepali Bhasha Prakasani Samiti for some time.

After 2007 BS, cutting the later part of his name 'Samsher Jangha Bahadur Rana,' he starting writing 'Sama'—meaning 'equal'—to show that all men were equal. During his service, he became the Director of Publicity Department and the Editor-in-Chief of the *Gorkhapatra*. When the Royal Nepal Academy—currently Nepal Academy—was established in 2014 BS, he became a member. Later he worked as the Vice Chancellor of the Academy. He was nominated a member of the Royal Assembly and served the country and society for some years.

There is a great contribution of him in Nepali language and literature. Given below are the books he wrote on different subjects:

Plays: 1. Mutuko Byatha, 2. Dhruva, 3. Mukunda Indira, 4. Prahlad, 5. Aandhabeg, 6. Bhakta-Bhanubhakta, 7. Ma, 8. Prempinda, 9. Amar Singh, 10. Tala-Maathi, 11. Amit Basana, 12. Tansenko Jhari, 13. Bhimsenko Aantya, 14. Swasni Manchhe, 15. Oo Mareki Chhaina.

Poems and Epic: 1. Aago ra Pani and, 2. Chiso Chulho.

Biography: 1. Mero Kavitako Aaradhana (part 1 and 2), 2. Hamra Rashtriya Bibhuti.

As stated above, Sama was basically a dramatist. He is often called the Shakespeare of Nepal. He developed new styles of rhyme in writing dramas. He was an excellent painter too.

He was honored with Pritivi Puraskar, a prize consisting of one hundred thousand rupees. He was the first Nepali to receive that prize. He passed away on 6 Shrawan 2038 BS.

■

Pundit Chhabilal Pokhrel

A single man can work in different fields: as a poet, critic, grammarian, essayist, autobiographer, researcher, political cadre, social worker, and educationalist etc. Chhabilal Pokhrel is an example of such a person. He is often called a 'pundit.' He did many things to uproot blind faith, conservatism and untouchability from the society.

Chhabilal was born on 1 Mangsir 1962 BS in Kachinde Village of Dhankuta District. His father's name was Bedanidhi Upadyaya Pokhrel and his mother's name, Arundhati. He was the second son of his parents.

Chhabilal learnt the alphabets from his well-educated father at home. He got married to Balmaya Bhandari in 1973 BS. At that time, he was only eleven years old.

At the age of fifteen, he started attending a school. There were not many schools at the time. So, he enrolled at the school of Hanuman Nagar of Saptari District, and studied as a boarder at the hostel run by the same school. After he cleared his intermediate from there, he went to Banaras of India and from there, he earned a postgraduate degree in 1990 BS.

With the thought that one should get to study any discipline of his or her choice, Chhabilal Pokhrel founded the J. P. Private School in Dhankuta in 1989 BS. In 1996 BS, the school was renamed Gokundeshowar High School. He opened another school in Sankhwasabha District too. After that in 2002 BS, he established a social institution called 'Sewa Samiti' in Dhankuta. In the same year, he moved to Dharan of Sunsari District. In Dharan, he founded the Multi-purpose Public High School in 2003 BS. At his initiative, Sharada Girls' School was established in 2004 BS. In the same year, he opened a library named Public Vidya Bhawan and an institution named Sanskrit Vidya Samvardhini Samiti. In 2005 BS, he opened Sri Ram Sanskrit School at Bijayapur of Dharan. Pindeshwar Sanskrit University was established in 2008 BS in Dharan with his support. At his initiative Mahendra Multiple Campus was opened in Dharan in 2009 BS. At every school and university he opened, he taught. He remained in the teaching profession till 2049 BS. This way, he taught for forty-one years altogether.

With a thought to transform the society, he taught Dalit students—considered untouchable—together with other non-Dalit ones at a school before 2007 BS. Giving a blow to the belief that women were not entitled to read the *Vedas*, he taught the *Vedas* to the women. He accepted inter-caste marriage inside his own family. He also showed the example that it was alright to get married with foreigners and with people of other religions. He was against the practice of child marriage. He also advocated widow re-marriage. He read the *Puranas* at houses of a Dalit for the first time. He administered *bratabandha*—initiation ritual for Hindu boys—to people of Rai and Limbu communities for the first time. In the past, the Brahmins and the Chhetris, considered high in the caste heirarchy, were not entitled to eat tomato, onion and garlic. Considering the belief senseless, he taught them to eat tomato, onion and garlic. He was the person who made the Dalits enter a temple in Nepal for the first time.

Chhabilal was also involved in politics. He took part in the movement against the Rana regime in 2007 BS. He was of the opinion that there should be a fair political environment in the country so as to ensure educational and social progress.

Chhabilal is a famous writer. In both Nepali and Sanskrit languages, he has written many books. Books he authored are as follows:

1. Muktachayanam, 2. Kaumudisar, 3. Mahatma Gandhi Tatha Astangayog ra Aadarsha Byavahar, 4. 2032 Sal Dharan Gosthiko Bibaranpatra, 5. Sankhyakarika, 6. Ishwar ra Byavahar, 7. Hamro Jaati Byavasta, 8. Ved ra Bhrama Niwaran, 9. Vedko Mukhya Peya Somarasbaare Bhram Niwaran ra Madyapanko Itihas, 10. Patanjal Yogsutra Byakhya, 11. Vaidik Siddhanta ra Manav Samaj, 12. Bhawataranga, 13. Hamro Dharma, 14. Vedadekhika Dharma ra Mathharoo, 15. Ishai Sampradaya: Ek Samiksha, 16. Samalochanako Kasima Devasur Sangram, 17. Tyo Yug: Bibechanatmak Adhyayan, 18. Aadhunik Drishtima Balmiki Ramayan, 19. Chhabilal Pokhrel, 20. Jatjati ra Sampradaya.

Besides these, hundreds of his articles and write-ups have been published in different books and magazines. If we publish them in collections, many books can be compiled.

Because of his remarkable contribution in writing and social service, Chhabilal Pokhrel was highly appreciated, honored and revered through felicitations and awards. He was awarded with Dr. Ambedkar Fellowship (1989) from India and Siksha Sewa Padak (2044), Social Service Prize (2052), Mahendra Pragya Puraskar (2053), and Kesar Singh Karki Khadgakumari Puraskar (2053). Nepal Writers' Assciation organized a chariot procession in his honor, and felicitated him with a ride across the city. Ancient Religion Service Committee, Pindeshwar Vidayapeeth, Gokundeshwar High School and Nepal Arya Samaj conferred upon him their due felicitation. He was also awared with Pratibha Prize. World Hindu Association, National Dalit Commission, B.P. Koirala Health Science Institute, Siddartha Banasthali Institute, and Ganeshman Singh Pratisthan felicitated him. Government of Nepal conferred upon him the title 'Gorkha Dakshinbahu Fourth' (2054). Apart from these titles, prizes and honors, he also received the title 'Hrisikalpa' from Yogi Naraharinath. Collecting the articles written on him by different authors of Nepal, a book named *Prasiddha Samajsevi Pundit Chhabilal Pokhrel Avinandan Grantha* has been published.

Chhabilal Pokhrel contributed immensely for his country. He breathed his last on 1st of Falgun 2056 at his own house in Dharan. At his death, many associations and institutions expressed their condolences. An institution named 'Chhabilal Pokhrel Pratisthan' has been established in honor of him. Though dead physically, he is still alive in the hearts of many Nepalese people as a legendary hero in the field of social development.

■

Chittadhar Hridaya: A Poetic Jewel

Chittadhar Hridaya is a prominent literary figure, who wrote in both Nepali and Newari languages. 'Hridya' is his pen-name, but his surname is Tuladhar. The nation has given him the title 'Kavikeshari'—a poetic jewel. He is one of the best-known poets of Newari language and literature.

Chittadhar Hridaya was born on 5 Jestha 1963 BS at Raktakali of Kathmandu. His father's name was Drabyadhar Tuladhar and his mother's name, Gyan Laxmi. He was serious in nature since his childhood days. Those days, there were no schools. So he did not get a chance to attend any. Whatever he read was through his personal efforts at home.

Hridaya was interested in reading and writing stories and poems since childhood. There were some books at his home. The books were about Gautam Buddha and Buddhist philosophy. By reading those books, he wished he could write such beautiful books. He gradually started writing stories and poems in Newari language. In 1982 BS, the first magazine of Newari language was printed from Kathmandu. Dharmadatta Dharmacharya was the editor of that magazine. The name of that magazine was *Buddhadharma wa Nepal Bhasa*. In that very magazine, Chittadhar Hridaya got his earliest poem "Buddhopaskaya Papdesana" published.

After knowing that Chittadhar Hridaya wrote wonderful poems. Poet Pundit Nisthananda Bajracharya, poet Siddidas Amatya, poet Yogbir Singh Kangsakar, and master Jagat Sundar Malla had encouraged him. He also went on writing poems. His neighbors used to tell him that 'a son of a merchant must do business; studying is some other people's task.' But his heart craved to read and write rather than get involved in business. He started thinking how to make people literate.

With a thought that all should get to study, he opened a small library in Kathmandu in 1968 BS. It was Nepal's first library. Mahakavi Laxmi Prasad Devkota was also in the group later. But the Rana rulers arrested all the members of the group and got them imprisoned. This incident is called 'Pustakalaya Kanda' or the library incident. Following the incident, educationalists, litterateurs, and intellectuals were threatened and some of them received severe tortures too. Chittadhar was sentenced to a jail term. He was accused of having a hand in the library incident. In fact, this had been done to put a stop in his writing in Newari language, because the Ranas did not like stories and poems written in Newari language.

But he was released from the jail soon. Inviting him to the palace, Prime Minister Juddha Samsher warned him against writing any other work in Newari language. But he did not give up serving his language.

Meanwhile, his mother died. Then, he wrote a poem in memory of his mother. The poem was titled 'Matribihin Balak'—a motherless child. But the Ranas misinterpreted it. They explained that the Newars were not allowed to use their mother tongue, and so, accused Chittadhar of violating the law. It was in the year of 1997. In the same year, four people involved in politics against Ranas were given death penalty, and some others were hurled into jail. Filing a case against him, the Ranas sent Chittadhar back into the jail, along with other political prisoners in Mangsir, 1997 BS. He was freed from jail in Kartik, 2002 BS.

In the jail, poets like Siddhi Charan Shrestha, Kedarman Byathit, Dharmaratna Yami and Hari Krishna Shrestha were his friends. They went on encouraging him not to give up writing. Because of that encouragement, he wrote a great epic, while still in the prison. *Sugat Saurav* is the name of the epic. It has 19 cantos, spread over 358 pages. There is no other epic of such prominence in Newari literature.

Even after he was released from prison with strict warning, Hridaya went on writing books. These are the books he has written:

Epic: 1.Sugat Saurav.

Children's literature: 1. Jhi Macha.

Story collection: 1. M'mi Man: Pau.

Research: 1. Jhigu Sahitya, 2. Nepal Bhasama Sahityaya Jaata:.

Felicitating his contribution in the field of literature, his fiftieth anniversary was organized and celebrated as a public festival. On that occasion, he was conferred with the title 'Sahityashiromani,' —Writer of Great Eminence—from the public level. King Mahendra honored him the title 'Kavikeshari' —Poetic Jewel—in 2013 BS. The government also provided him a monthly allowance.

In the same year, as the vice president of Nepalese Cultural Circle, he visited People's Republic of China. The monthly allowance he received was increased during the time of King Birendra. Among Newari litterateurs, he was the first to receive a royal tribute.

Writer of more than three dozen books, this poet, story writer, essayist, editor, critic, and explorer, died on 26 Jestha, 2039 BS at his own home. With his death, Nepal lost an influential man.

In the tenth year of his death, a postal stamp was issued by the government of Nepal in his honor. His birth centenary was celebrated in 2062 BS. His statue has been erected on the ground of Ratna Rajya Secondary School, Mid-Baneshwar, Kathmandu. Still, researches are going on about him. He is a great hero of our country.

■

Novelist Roop Narayan Singh

Novelist Roop Narayan Singh has a great name in Nepali literature. Writing just a few novels, he is the one among the much talked-about litterateurs of Nepal. A single novel made him renowned. His is the first ever novel that depicts the life and suffering of Nepali people living in India.

Roop Narayan was born in a Chhetri family of Kunwar Khadka on 24 Magh 1963 BS. His forefathers had lived in Kharsang of India migrating from Nepal. His family was a high class and a wealthy one. The Kunwar Khadkas, who had been to Kharsang, had begun to write 'Singh' as their surname after they reached there. Roop Narayan's family lived at Sipahidhura of Kharsang.

Roop Narayan was sharp-minded in study since his very young age. He was initially admitted to a primary school in Kharsang. After he grew up, he was enrolled at a public school in Darjeeling. He did his matriculation from there. By studying law, he developed a flair for a legal job from a very young age. Law, you know, is a discipline studied by people who want to become lawyers. That's why, after passing matriculation, Roop Narayan shared his desire to study law with his father. To fulfill his son's desire, his father sent him to study further in Calcutta.

He entered the University of Calcutta in 1982 B.S at the I.A. level. Alongside, he had a deep interest in litetature too—a flair he had carried in him since his early age. But, because of the hard times he was facing, he did not immediately write anything.

During his student days, he kept traveling between Culcutta and Kharsang. During that time, he read English, Hindi and Bengali stories. Those stories inspired him to write stories in his mother tongue – Nepali. He felt like doing something for his mother tongue. And then, he began to think what he could do for the development of his mother tongue.

Soon an idea of publishing a magazine of Nepali language occurred to him. He, therefore, started a literary magazine *Khoji* in his own editorship.

As he was doing his I.A., Roop Narayan wrote two stories in 1983 BS. The stories he wrote were published in *Khoji*. He was just twenty years old at the time.

He earned his B.A. degree from Calcutta University. And then, he did B.L. too from there. He returned to Darjeeling with an objective to practise law. In 1989 BS, he chose the profession of a lawyer, and started dealing with cases in a court.

When he was twenty-nine years old, he wrote a novel named *Bhramar*. Nine years later, he began writing stories. The novel was printed in 1993 BS. Rudra Raj Pandey's novel *Roopamati* had been printed in 1991 BS from Kathmandu. Just two years after Pandey's novel was published, Roop Narayan's novel *Bhramar* was published from Darjeeling. In Nepali literature, these two novels are known as the foundations of modern fiction.

Like *Roopmati, Bhramar* became a milestone for the people within and outside Nepal. Soon after its publication, Roop Narayan began writing another novel named *Bijuli* but he couldn't complete that.

In 2005 BS, Roop Narayan again wrote a few more stories. His stories were published in the magazines *Sharada, Gorkha, Sahityashrot, Bharati* and so on. Soon, he himself became the chief editor of *Bharati*. In that magazine, some parts of his half-done novel *Bijuli* were published. Later in 2007 BS, *Katha Nawaratna*, a collection of his nine stories, was published. His published books are:

Novel: 1. Bhramar.

Collection of the Stories: 1. Katha Nawaratna.

There are two other stories, which have not been included in *Nawaratna* but published in different magazines. The novel *Bijuli* has not been published yet.

During his days, Roop Narayan was active in literary field. He even became a part of an academic movement, with support form the Nepalese who lived in Darjeeling, demanding that Nepali subject should be included in the national curriculum. The institution 'Nepali Literary Conference' led the movement. He was also a member of that institution. He worked for many other social associations and institutions besides 'Nepali Literary Conference.'

Roop Narayan was a scholarly and dignified man. He was of strict nature, and couldn't tolerate anybody's tyranny. He feared no one. His heart was soft, and he was emotional. He would be sad at others' suffering.

When he was just forty-eight years old, he became isolated from his family. Due to this, pessimistic thoughts developed in him. In the same situation, he passed away in 2011 BS in Darjeeling.

Although he is dead, Roop Narayan is living in his immortal work *Bhramar*. His contribution has become an source of inspiration for all the Nepalese people. He has become a bright star in the field of Nepali language and literature.

■

Poet Yuddha Prasad Mishra

Hamro bhainsi bubu dinchha
Bubu chahi arule kinchha
Ani pachhi dhindo nistai hunchha
Bahini runchhe, bhai runchha.

[Our buffalo gives us milk and it is sold in the market. And then, children cry because there is no milk with dhindo—porridge prepared from boiled maize flour or millet flour.]

Aadhi aayo, aasina aayo
Janti basne gharai udayo
Syalko bihe bhangbhang bhungbhung
Aaja Asar bholi Saaun
Ghampani ghampani syalko bihe
Kukur janti biralo bahun.

[Wind-storm and hail-storm blew away the shed where the marriage-goers stayed. The wedding of a wolf is nothing but a hullabaloo. It is Asar today and Srawan tomorrow. Sunshine and rain mark the wedding of a fox. The dog joins the wedding procession, while the cat plays the priest.]

The above beautiful poem for children was authored by poet Yuddha Prasad Mishra. Mishra was born on 27 Paush 1964 BS at Sumlingtar of Bhaktapur District. His father's name was Rudra Prasad Mishra and mother's Geeta Kumari.

The economic condition of Mishra's family was not quite good. It was engaged in farming. There were not many schools at the time. So, he didn't get to attend one. Whatever he read, he did it at home. And whatever he knew, he knew from the practical life he faced.

Though he couldn't study at a school, he was quite brilliant. Hence, he got a job by the time he became a young adult. Rana regime was prevalent at the time. He got a job from the favor of the Ranas.

Yuddha Prasad used to write poems even as he attended his job. He began to compose poems from a very young age. He would instantly write a poem if he found anything that touched his heart. His poem titled "Vidyarthi Siksya" was published in *Gorkhapatra* in 1988 BS. This was his first published poem. The poem was very beautiful. So, many people appreciated him. He was encouraged to compose more poems.

Yuddha Prasad initially wrote poems about forests, birds, rivers, Himalayas, hills and so on. For writing a poem titled "Chara," he received a cash prize from the then 'Nepali Bhasha Prakashini Samiti, a reputed literary institution. After that, he wrote poems resisting the immoral activities and conducts that were rampant in the society. Those poems were revolutionary in nature.

His revolutioanry poems invited him many risks. He was accused of writing agaisnt the establishment. A case was filed against him and he was proved guilty. He was kept in prison in Birgunj. It is an incident of 2004 BS.

Yuddha Prasad came in contact with litterateur Shyam Prasad Sharma while he was in prison in Birgunj. They both continued writing poems in the jail. Yuddha Prasad wrote verses and read them out to Shyam Prasad, while the latter wrote essays and read out to Yuddha Prasad. So, their writing turned out to be excellent.

After he was released from jail, he came back to Bhaktapur. Again, another case was filed against him. His house was ransacked. His eldest son left the house when it was robbed. Till today, his whereabouts have remained a mystery.

A collosal political change took place in Nepal in 2017 BS. King Mahendra suspended all parliamentary practices and imposed Panchayat rule under his direct dicatorial leadership. Yuddha Prasad didn't like the move. He wrote poems resisting the undesired change. For this, he was, once again chased away from Bhaktapur. He, taking his family, went to India and lived there. He wrote poems regularly even there.

Among his poems, the poems entitled "Suryaghatma," "Chara," "Charkhandiko Khoj," "Bankalima," "Jabiko Chara," "Jalan," "Kam Paun," "Hami," "Aawara," "Mero Yougko Chhati," "Mudbhed," and "Bhoka ra Nanga Utha" and so on are quite famous.

He would carve poems to touch the heart of the common people. An example of the type of poems he wrote in given below:

Krantikari charitrako veer swabhimani
Dekhaideu timi pani Nepaliko pani
Badhdai jau yatharthako dharatal mathi
Manabiya nyaya khojdai ladhdai jau sathi.

[Just show your courage because you are a Nepali : bold, dignified and rich in revolutionary characteristics. Just go friends, seeking and fighting for humanitarian justice based on ground reality.]

Yuddha Prasad passed many years in India writing such revolutionary poems. Later, his sons and daughters returned to Kathmandu. But, he didn't. His offspring stayed at Phayafal of Kathmandu in a rented home. His sons sold medicine at Dundikhel. The daughters attended schools. However, he continued to stay in India.

Yuddha Prasad came back to Kathmandu only in 2040 BS. He lived for some years in rented rooms in different places of the city. Later, after his sons built a house at Gatthaghar of Bhaktapur, he moved there to live with his sons. There, even in his old age, he continued writing poems.

The books he wrore are these:

Collection of Poems: 1. Chara, 2. Badhi, 3. Yuddha Prasad Mishraka Kabitaharoo.

Short Epic: 1. Mukti Ramayan Aranyakanda, 2. Mukta Sudama.

Collection of Stories: 1. Amar Katha.

Editing: 1. Mukti Morcha.

Apart from these books, many other stories, poems and essays Yuddha Prasad wrote have been published in many different magazines. If all these are collected, other books can be published.

Yuddha Prasad had a desire to author a long epic. But his desire could not be fulfilled because he did not find time. He also wrote poems for children. Those poems were published in different magazines. But, a separate book of his poems has not been published yet. One of his poems for children runs like this:

Uthchhu, padhchhu, kapada pherchhu, safa suggar bhai aina herchhu
Tifinsathko jhola bhirchu, skul janchhu, tam tam tam
Thorai khelchhu, dherai padhchu, paath nabirsi aghi aghi badchhu
Nabhai chhaddina ma pani first
Ko bhanda ko chha kam, skul janchu tam tam tam.

[I get up early in the morning and I read for some time. I change my dress and look into the mirror, being neat and clean. I carry my bag with tiffin box and I go to school merrily. I play for some time, but read more. I learn all the lessons by heart because I want to stand first. I am also capable. I go to school merrily.]

Yuddha Prasad talked about literature to those who came to visit him. He used to opine that literature should represent good things. He thought that immoral endeavors should be discouraged whereas virtuous activities should be admired.

Yuddha Prasad was felicitated on 23 Bhadra 2041 BS in Kathmandu. A special volume of literary magazine was published in his name in Jestha, 2042 BS. Later, he fell ill and was admitted to Bir Hospital. At that time, he was announced to be the winner of Krishna Mani Sahitik Puraskar. He accepted the prize even if he was ill. While receiving treatment at Bir Hospital, he breathed his last on the morning of 6 Falgun 2047 BS. He was eighty-four years old at that time.

After his death, his statue has been erected in his birth place Sumlingtar. A literary institution called Yuddha Prasad Mishra Puraskar and Prakasan Guthi has been established in his commemoration. The very institute publishes a literary magazine named *Yuddha* in his name. His other compositions are being searched for. The collection of poems called *Yuddha Prasadka Kabita* has been published by the institution, albeit posthumously.

Yuddha Prasad Mishra's poems are of the types to be very much adored by poor people. That's why he is often called the 'poet of the poor people.' Despite the fact that he is dead, his poems are left with us. We always find his contemplations or thoughts alive in the poems. He is an honest muse of our country.

■

Linguist Hari Prasad Gorkha Rai

Hari Prasad Gorkha Rai was born in Nagaland, Kohima of India on 25 Ashad 1965 BS. His father's name was Dharma Raj Rai and his mother's name Yashoda Rai. Many years back, his grandfather had migrated to India from Okhaldunga of Nepal. After sometime, Dhan Raj Rai also went to stay with his father. So, Hari Prasad was born in India.

At that time in Kohima— where they lived—even a single school had not been opened. So, when he was a small boy, Hari Prasad did not get to study. Later, a Bengali school was opened and he was enrolled in grade one at the age of fifteen. Six years was deducted from his actual age while admitting. A teacher named Mitrasen Mahant taught him there. The very teacher taught him the idea that one should maintain his original identity. That's why, he tagged the title 'Gorkhali' to his name, as he was an Indian of Nepali origin by birth. This was an attempt by him to assert his identity as a Gorkhali, the martial class of Nepali warriors. This was the proof that he loved his fatherland very much.

Hari Prasad studied Bengali at his school. After he reached the secondary level, he studied Hindi too. It was not difficult for him to learn Nepali language because it was their family language. Due to his keen interest in painting, he used to draw pictures of Nepali writers. In 1992 BS, he accomplished his bachelor degree in English and Philosophical Studies. He also accomplished a degree in Hindi literature. After some time, he began teaching at Nagaland High School. Then, he got appointed as the Assistant Station Director at All India Radio, Orissa. In 2014

BS, he started working for All India Radio, Guwahati. Two years later, he began a program of Nepali language from the same radio station. He resigned from the job in 2025 BS.

Hari Prasad wrote essays, stories and poems since his childhood. His first composition was an essay titled "Ma Nepali Hoon." That essay was published in *Gorkha Sewak* in 1988 BS. His compositions were also published in *Tarun Gorkha, Bharati, Gorkha, Udaya, Gorkha Sansar* and *Himadri*. In *Sharada* his stories were published with the name Mrs. Junumaya Rai. He also wrote in Assamese language. His first poem in Assamese was "Sahisnuta" published in *Jeuti*, a magazine of the Assamese language. His compositions were also published in magazines like *Ahwan, Akan* and *Banhi*.

Following are the published books of Hari Prasad Gorkha Rai:

Collection of stories: 1. Bipanapal, 2. Yaha Badanam Hunchha, 3. Hari Prasad Gorkha Raika Kathaharoo.

Collection of poems: 1. Babari, 2. Manchariko Boli.

Novels: 1. Madan.

History: 1. Nagalandko Chheukuna.

Autobiography: 1. Pharkera Herda.

Dictionary: 1. Nepali-Hindi Dictionary, 2. Nepali-Aashami Dictionary, 3. Nepali-Bengali Dictionary, 4. Hindi-Karbi (Mikir) Dictionary, 5. Rongmei-Hindi Dictionary, 6. Maram-Hindi Dictionary, 7. Marig-Hindi Dictionary, 8. Garo-Hindi Dictionary, 9. Assamiya-Hindi Dictionary, 10. Nepali-Hindi Swayam Sikshan, 11. Meiri-Hindi Dictionary.

In Assamiya Language: 1. Assamar Janjati.

Hari Prasad also edited the handwritten Nepali papers *Sawarsati, Pashupati Birna, Ek Thunga Dui Phool* and *Jagriti*. Besides these, he also translated a few Assamese stories and novels into Nepali. His book *Assamar Janjati* is taught at M.A. level at Guwahati University.

Hari Prasad was the founder of Pashupati Association, Tarun Association, and Gorkhas and Other People's Union. He was also a member of the Assam Literature Congress. He worked for many years as a Nepali consultant at Sahitya Academy, New Delhi.

Hari Prasad received a literary pension of one thousand rupees per month from Assam State Government until his death. He had receieved Bhasa Sangrami Pratik, Padma Dhungana Smriti Puraskar, Bhasa Manyata Diwas Puraskar, and Parasmani Tatha Agam Shingh Giri Smriti Puraskar from India. He received Madan Smarak Byakhyanmala and Jagadambashree awards (2052) from Nepal. He is considered a pioneer of modern Nepali literature in the north-eastern part of India. In many books and papers of Nepal and India, articles about him have been published. Many researches have been done about him.

In the later period of his life, Hari Prasad stayed with his eldest daughter. He died at the age of ninety-seven on 28 Kartik 2062 BS in Assam. Even after his death, he is living in the hearts of thousands of Nepalese and Indian people who read and write Nepali language. The contribution he has made for Nepali language and literature is unforgettable.

■

Badarinath Bhattarai: A Writer of Merit

Nirdhalai kichmich gare paap thulo
*   thaharchha*
Aaphujastaisanga ta bhidinda
*   yuddhako khel banchha.*

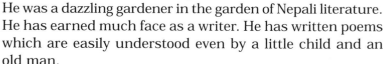

[Oppressing the meek ones leads but to a sin.

Fighting with the equals, a game of war it is.]

Badarinath Bhattarai is the poet who teaches us this lofty idea. He was a dazzling gardener in the garden of Nepali literature. He has earned much face as a writer. He has written poems which are easily understood even by a little child and an old man.

He was born in Kartik, 1965 BS at Indra Chowk of Kathmandu. His father's name was Damodarnath Bhattarai. He built a house at Nagpokhari, Naxal of Kathmandu. He lived in that house. He had Sashtri, a degree in Sanskrit equivalent to the bachelor's degree and Acharya, equivalent to master's degree in religious studies from Banaras of India.

He was a very straightforward and gentle boy since childhood. He was also interested in religious activities. He felt that reading books makes a man scholar. So, he would always study different books. He would often stand first or second in the examination.

Badrinath was deeply pained by many anomalies in the society. He would think how he could change such an immoral society into a better one.

While staying in India for his higher education, he got acquainted with many renowned people and authors there.

He felt like writing stories and poems. Upon finishing his master's degree, he came back to Kathmandu and got engaged in a job at Nepali Bhasha Prakashini Samiti. He got the job of Chief Pundit there.

While working there, he got acquainted with many famous litterateurs of Nepal. And then, he began to write stories and poems. He also began to translate books written in Sanskrit language.

At the time, *Sharada*, the literary magazine, was being published from Kathmandu. That magazine was edited by Riddhi Bahadur Malla. A poem translated from Sanskrit into Nepali by him was published in the very magazine in 1998 BS. At the time, he was just 33 years old. After this, he carried on translating. He also did not abandon writing original stories, poems, and articles in his own Nepali language.

Badarinath believed that everyone should study and become a scholar. So, he would explain people about the importance of education. He used to say that we should not leave our ancient religion; we should not give up the good tradition practiced in the past and we should remove immoral practices. He advised people that we should feel proud of the work our ancestors did and passed on to us; and we too should do such worthy works which can uphold the glory in our society.

These 34 books are, among his works, both original ones and edited one:

Collection of the poems: 1. Pauranik Kahani, 2. Baidik Kahani, 3. Aitihasik Kahani, 4. Pauranik Katha (part 1), 5. Pauranik Katha (part 2).

Short Epic: 1. Sindhuliko Jhalak.

Collection of Essays: 1. Pachchis Prabandha, 2. Prabandha Pallav.

Articles and Reviews: 1. Sanskrit Sahityako Sinhawalokan, 2. Ishwarko Sewa Kasari Garne?, 3. Ishwar Kina Manne?, 4. Udyog Dhandha.

Language: 1. Anuvad Prakashika, 2. Anubad Bodhini

Religion and Culture: 1. Aatma Puran 2. Dharmabodha (part 1), 3. Dharmabodha (part 2) 4. Dharmabodha (part 3) 5. Dharmabodha (part 4) and 6. Dharmabodha (part 5)

Translation: 1. Kadambari, 2. Stutidhara (part 1), 3. Stitutidhara (part 2), 4. Shaakari Amritdhara.

Editing: 1. Vidhya Gita, 2. Hari Stuti, 3. Gajendra Moksha, 4. Ram Gita, 5. Brahma Gita, 6. Devi Gita, 7. Hamsha Gita, 8. Bhikshu Gita, 9. Yog Bashistharas.

Besides these, many of his stories, poems, plays, articles, essays and criticisms have been published in miscellany. By the end of his life, through spiritual meditation, he had discovered his true self.

Serving a lot to Nepali language and literature, he became a member of Education Council for a few years. He taught Sanskrit at Tribhuvan University and Balmiki Vidhyapeeth for many years.

He was conferred the prestigious Gunaraj Puraskar, a literary prize, for editing a book called 'Yog Bashistharas.' He also won Bedhanidhi Puraskar in 2045 BS. He was conferred the title 'Sanskrit Manisi', the master of Sanskrit.

Badarinath edited some works of Laxmi Prasad Devkota, the great poet. He was considered extremely good in writing prefaces. In this way, he worked for Nepali language and literature very hard, translating books, writing prefaces, writing introductions of authors, and teaching in the colleges. Badarinath, plain natured, explicit in writing, and quite amiable, has now become a model of high excellence for our society as well as for our school-going children.

He left this world on 4 Magha 2052 BS. Though his earthly body is no more with us, the books he left with us will always inspire us to become worthy citizens and to make our society better.

For teaching us moral lessons in a language understandable to everyone, and for bringing up to us many stories from the scriptures, Badarinath will always be remembered with high respect or esteem.

■

Storywriter Bhawani Bhikshu

The story titled "Tyo Pheri Pharkela"— He Might Come Back— is a very popular story in Nepali literature. The story was written by Bhawani Bhikshu.

An author famous in the genres of stories, poems, and novels, renowned litterateur Bhawani Bhikshu's real name is Bhawani Prasad Gupta. He was born on 21 Jestha 1966 BS in a village called Goti of Kapilbastu district of Lumbini Zone. His father's name was Indra Prasad Gupta. His mother tongue was 'Awadhi.' He had studied Nepali, Hindi, English, and Urdu.

He was born in an ordinary family, not in a wealthy one. After coming to Kathmandu from Kapilbastu, he had to struggle extremely hard just for survival. The poor economic condition troubled him very much. However, he was a learned man, patient, bold and valorous. So, despite all these sufferings, he did not lose his heart. He did not give up literary pursuits. He carried on writing stories, novels, and poems even when he was engaged in job.

He was born in the Tarai region. So, he did 'Sahitya Kulbhusan' in Hindi. However, he had much of his general education in Nepali language.

After he came to Kathmandu, he became the editor of the popular magazine *Sharada*. Seeing his qualification, he was offered the editorship. At the time, the editor of the' *Sharada* was Riddhi Bahadur Malla. He was also a litterateur. He knew the caliber of Bhawani Bhikshu.

Bhikshu's first story is 'Manab'. It was published in the *Sharada* in 1995 BS. Many stories and poems of him had been published in the same magazine.

Bhikshu was of dark complexion and rather short-built. However, he was a lover of beauty. He would speak with weighty words and think gravely while having conversation with people. He never pronounced audacious words from his mouth.

Ten books he wrote have been published. Among them are four collections of stories, three collections of poems and three novels.

Following are the books he wrote:

Collection of stories: 1.Gunakesari, 2.Maiya Saheb, 3. Aawarta, 4. Abantar.

Collection of the poems: 1. Chhaya, 2. Prakash, 3. Pariskhar.

Novels: 1 Subhadra Bajai, 2. Aagat, 3. Pipe no. 2.

While writing, Bhikshu would at first think in Hindi and then write down in Nepali. The corpus he wrote has proven to be a great achievement for Nepali literature today.

He became the Director General of Communication Department from 2008 BS to 2013 BS.

The Royal Nepal Academy was established in 2014 BS with an objective to develop and promote Nepali language and literature. Bhikshu became a member of that Academy. He also became the full time member of the Academy, later. Taking charge of its Prose Department's work, he performed plenty of works. From his efforts, the Academy expanded its contact and communication to different places outside the country.

He served Nepali literature in an appreciable manner. He got Tribhuvan Puraskar in 2036 BS. He was conferred

Madan Puraskar in 2032 BS for his novel *Aagat*. He is sometimes called a mysticist novelist.

Bhikshu died on 4 Baisakh 2038 BS in Kathmandu. After his death, the government issued a postal stamp in his name.

■

Great Poet Laxmi Prasad Devkota

Haatakaa mailaa sunakaa thailaa,
ke garnu dhanale?
Saaga ra sisno khayeko besa
aanandi manale.

[In these famous lines from *Muna Madan*, the poet says that bags of gold are like filth of your hand; there's no meaning, accumulating a lot of pelf. Best is the life that lives on greens and nettle leaves with full contentment.]

Children, do you know who wrote the above poem? If you don't know, I will tell you. The lines were written by Mahakavi of Nepal—the greatest poet of all times—Laxmi Prasad Devkota.

Devkota was born in 1966 BS in the month of Kartik. His father's name was Til Madav Devkota and his mother's Amar Rajya Laxmi Devi. His name at birth was Tirtha Madav Devkota. But, it was decided that he would be named Laxmi Prasad as he was born on the night of Laxmi Puja—the fourth day of the second greatest festival Tihar of the Hindu people.

Devkota was badly attacked by dysentery when he was four years old. At that time, everyone had become hopeless of his survival. He was treated carefully. Ultimately, a magician advised his family to feed him 'Jungali Sel.' After feeding the Jungali Sel, the dysentery was cured. The story Jungali Sel at his family is still famous.

His basic education began in Sanskrit. He was sharp-minded from a very small age. He completed his study from Kathmandu and Patan. He first studied science and switched on to literature and law. He earned the degrees of B.A. and B.L. Though he pursued M.A. in English literature for some time, he could not complete because of economic crisis at home.

He had the habit of writing poems from a very young age. The first poem, the one he wrote at the age of ten, opens like this:

Ghanaghor dukha sagar sansar jana bhai
Nagare ghamanda kahilyai marnu chha hamilai.

[Brother, the world is a sea of misery. Do not pride in yourself; we all will surely die.]

Mahakavi Devkota was a versatile poet. It is really difficult to explicate his mastermind. He wrote many books devoting his entire life to literature. Books he wrote are as follows:

Short epic: 1. Muna Madan, 2. Kunjini, 3. Sitaharan, 4. Mhendo, 5. Basanti, 6. Luni, 7. Rajkumar Pravakar, 8. Ravan-Jatayu Yuddha.

Poems: 1. Nawaras, 2. Manoranjan, 3. Bhikhari, 4. Putali, 5. Chhahara, 6. Chilla Patharoo.

Long epic: 1. Shakuntal, 2. Sulochana, 3. Bankusum, 4. Maharana Pratap.

Plays: 1. Krisibala, 2. Sabitri-Satyavan.

Essays: 1. Laxmi Nibandha Sangraha, 2. Prasiddha Nibandha Sangraha.

Novel: 1. Champa.

Thus, with different works of high worth, he enriched the storehouse of Nepali literature. He was titled Mahakavi, the great poet, because he wrote a big corpus of epics. He became Mahakavi because of his extra-ordinary genius.

Once he began writing, his pen would not stop. And virtually speaking, he was Veda Vyas of Nepal.

Laxmi Prasad was the devotee of Goddess Saraswati, the goddess of knowledge. But Laxmi, the goddess of wealth, was never on his side. Poverty would always bother him. Devkota used to smoke a lot. So, he suffered from many disease resulting from that.

Devkota held a job at Translation Council and becoming a professor he taught at Tri-Chandra College. He would always keep his life busy.

He headed for India in 2004 BS. He edited the magazine *Yugvani* there. Through Nepali poems, he worked to bring awareness and dynamism in people. He also wrote revolutionary poems. Devkota also took profound interest in writing poems for children. One example is:

Natipnu hera kopila
Nachudnu papa lagdachha
Nachyatnu phoola naani ho!
Daya ra dharma bhaagdachha.

[Do not pick buds, children
That's a sin, you know!
Pick not the blossoms, either
Pity and virtue shall desert you.]

Devkota became the Education Minister in 2014 BS. Still, his nature remained the same. His economic condition did not improve. He also became the member of Royal Nepal Academy.

Eventually, a man must die once he is born. Other things can be avoided; death never. Dreadful diseases like cancer attacked Devkota, one of the most proficient personalities of Nepali literature. He was treated not only in Nepal, but also abroad. But it turned out worthless. He died in 2016 BS in the month of Bhadra. At the time of his death he said, "After I die, except for *Muna Madan,* you can burn all my books." Likewise, he acknowledged the existence of God at the end of his life saying, "I subsume in the void as void itself. Now I see, the only one so eternal is Krishna, the Ultimate."

After his death, Royal Nepal Academy honored him, with Tribhuvan Puraskar. He was also honored for 'Yogantakari Sahityasewa,' an epoch-making service to literature.

Like *Muna Madan*, the most popular of his epics, Poet Devkota is enshrined in the hearts of Nepali people with unbreakable bonds of love. Even people outside Nepal read and appreciate his great works. Devkota is perhaps the best internationally known writer of Nepal. A few works he wrote in English and those that were translated by skilled translators later, have made Laxmi Prasad Devkota and international literary figure. This is a matter of pride for all of us.

■

Historical Novelist Tukaraj Mishra

Tukaraj Mishra was a novelist. A novelist is a person who writes novels. A novel is a long story about people's experience or imagination. The author imagines much of the story in a novel, though he might borrow facts from history and other real-life happenings.

The first historical novel of Nepali language is *Rajbandhaki*. Tukaraj Mishra is the author of this novel.

Tukaraj Mishra was born in Falgun, 1966 BS at Tarkutar of Lamjung District. His father's name was Dilli Krishna Mishra and his mother's name Tika Laxmi. His father died when he was only eight. His family migrated from Tarkutar in 1980 BS. At that time, Tukaraj was fourteen. His mother came to Dhobidhara of Kathmandu with her children. They built a house there. And then they became inhabitants of Kathmandu.

Tukaraj Mishra learned the alphabets from his father. He did not leave his study even after his father died. Reading brilliantly, he earned himself the title of '*Hindi Sahityabhushan*' a title equivalent to bachelor's degree in Hindi.

Four years after he came to Kathmandu, he started working in a government office from the age of eighteen since 1984 BS. He got a job at the then Kumari Chok office to guard over the hillside. His salary was eleven rupees per month. And then he served in different offices in different capacities. He worked for forty-six years altogether. In 2029 BS, he was made the auditor at the Auditor General's office. In the same year, he got retirement from that position.

Among the poems he wrote, the first composition is "Sunma Sugandha," a problem-solving kind of a poem. This was the first time he had written a complete verse. That poem was published in *Sharada* in 1992 BS. After that, his literary pen never stopped.

Tukaraj wrote a novel in collaboration with his brother Padmaraj Mishra. *Rajbandhaki* is the name of the novel. That novel was published in 1996 BS. It drew a huge attention as it was the first novel jointly written by more than one author in the history of Nepali literaure. Many incidents of Rana times had been depicted in the novel. That is why the novel became highly demanded.

The appreciation of the novel gave a big encouragement to Tukaraj and his brother. They immediately wrote another novel *Ramkrishna Kunwar Rana*. It was published in 1999 BS. Everybody appreciated the work. They had written the novel adopting the events of history as its subject matter. Nobody had written such a novel before. Readers liked both the novels quite a lot because they got a text to read about curious incidents from inside the palace of the Ranas.

But the Ranas' henchmen did not like the descriptions narrated in the novel. So Tukaraj was accused of infidelity. It was announced that Tukaraj was not worthy of holding a job and writing anything. Unnecessary and false rumors about him were created and spread. Depressed, he did not publish any other book for a long time.

The Rana regime ended in 2007 and democracy was reinstated. Soon, Tukaraj published two short epics named *Nepal Aamako Krandan* and *Buddha Pariwarko Krandan* in 2013 BS. He also wrote a book named *Shresta Siksha*. His another historical novel was published in 2048 BS. The name of that novel is *Ridi ra Ranchi: Hansdai-Rudai*. He also wrote a book named *Mero Anubhootima Rudraraj Pandey* in 2051 BS. Books he has written include the following:

Novels: 1.Rajbandhaki, 2. Ram Krishna Kunwar Rana, 3. Ridi ra Ranchi: Hansdai-Rudai.

Shot epics: 1. Nepal Aamako Krandan, 2. Buddha Pariwarko Krandan.

Memoir: 1. Mero Anubootima Rudraraj Pandey.

Law: 1. Shresta Siksha, 2. Shresta Sambandha, 3. Adalat Sambandha.

Apart from these, collecting his compositions written separately and compiling them into books is still not done. If *Bhanubhakta ra Motiramko Samalochanatmak Jeevani*, including *Mero Aatmakatha* and *Teen Devi* (novel) and other manuscripts are published, the field of Nepali literature will become tremendously rich.

Tukaraj has received some rewards and felicitation for his contribution to the field of literature. He was crowned with 'Uttam Kunwar Puraskar' in 2048 BS for his novel *Ridi ra Ranchi: Hansdai-Rudai*. He received 'Rudraraj Aatirikta Puraskar' in 2051 BS for his research on Rudraraj Pandey, the novelist. Since 2052 BS, 'Sita Ram Sahitya Pratisthan' gave him an allowance of one thousand rupees per month for his life. He was also awarded with Vedanidhi Puraskar in 2053 BS for his service to literature for more than fifty years.

Nepal Government conferred upon him the title of 'Rastriya Pratibha Puraskar' in 2058 BS. On the occasion of the golden jubilee of Nepali Sahitya Mandir and Nepali Education Council he was felicitated. He was also felicitated by Khil Sharma Rajeevlochan Joshi Smarak Pratisthan in 2057 BS. In 2054 BS, a researcher from Tribhuvan University conducted a research "Tukaraj Mishra: Biography, Personality and Works of Art."

Tukaraj Mishra passed away on 19 Paush 2060 BS at the age of ninety-four at his own residence. Nepali literature lost a rare novelist who wrote historical novels for the first time in Nepali literature. He is a distinguished star of our literary field and his contribution to it will be remembered forever.

■

Editor and Litterateur Kashi Bahadur Shrestha

All the Nepalese will have to remember litterateur Kashi Bahadur Shrestha, who served Nepali language and literature even by living in Banaras, outside Nepal. He remarkably contributed to introducing Nepali language and literature among the Indians.

His ancestral house was at Tibukuche tole of Bhaktapur District. As his family belonged to business class, they would be going to different places. His father had lived in Banaras of India for the same purpose. He would deal in *kesar* – a part of flower pistil, *kusturi* – a kind of musk deer fragrance, and *jawaharat* – jewelries. In course of business, he would be traveling to different big cities of India.

Kashi's father had a cottage in Banaras. Banaras is also called Kashi. He was born in 1986 BS on Krishna Janastami – the eighth day of the solar fortnight in the month of Bhadra. His parents Ganesh Bahadur Shrestha and Bishnu Maya named the boy Kashi Bahadur because he was born in Kashi.

Kashi gradually kept growing up. When he was four years old, his father began to teach him at home. After some time, he was enrolled at a local school. He would go to the school and study laboriously. Meanwhile, his mother died. He was only nine at the time. He deeply sank in bereavement at his mother's demise. He was brought up by his father solely with great care. He didn't have to be helpless though his mother was no longer. His father arranged his marriage at the age of thirteen.

Kashi continued with his study. He passed his grade ten examination from Queen's College affiliated to Upper India Education Board of Banaras. And then, he joined I.A. program. However, he couldn't carry on his study because of his business. Staying at home and visiting libraries, he often studied Hindi, Bengali and English literature. But fate had it so; his father also died after some time. Kashi was twenty two years old at the time. So, he had to take the burden of the family on his own shoulders from a very young age.

Kashi would be traveling to different cities of India in the process of business. So, he became familiar with many top litterateurs of that country. His intimacy grew with Bharatendu Harischandra and Munsi Premchand in Banaras. He was influenced from both of them. He consequently determined to work for Nepali language and literature.

Kashi never held a job. He went on with business. He began to write literature alongside business. He wrote books and edited works written by others. He also got books and magazines published. He edited books written in Nepali language, managed to get published, and helped to promote. He also published a literary magazine.

Initially, he would write stories in Hindi language. His stories would be published in the magazines *Kamalini*, *Rangabhumi*, *Aaj* and so on in India. Later, his friend Anand Bahadur Shrestha requested him to write stories in Nepali; he then started to write stories, essays and novels in Nepali.

From the month of Falgun in 1993 BS, he started publishing a literary magazine named *Udaya*. In due course, he also launched literary magazines *Sharada* and *Udaya* that pioneered the history of literary journalism in Nepal. *Udaya* was the first Nepali literary magazine published from Banaras and, the third literary magazine of Nepali language.

Kashi published a novel named *Usha* in 1995 BS and a novel named *Bachan* in 2001 BS. *Udaya* magazine was closed in the meantime due to financial crisis. But as soon as he had money, he resumed the publication of *Udaya*. He regularly published it till 2024 BS. He also published *Tota Mainako Katha* as a collection of stories.

Kashi's published works are these:

Novel: 1. Usha, 2. Bachan.

Collection of Stories: 1. Tota Mainako Katha.

Editing: 1. Udaya.

Besides these, collections of many stories and articles in Nepali and Hindi languages, written by Kashi Bahadur Shrestha, are yet to be published. He had prepared a collection of stories named *Graduate*. But the collection has remained unpublished yet.

In recognition of his contribution to Nepali language and literature, Literary Journalist Association felicitated Kashi Bahadur in 2040 BS He was awarded with Madan Smarak Byakhyan Puraskar in 2046 BS by Bidyadharma Pracharani Samiti of Banaras.

Kashi Bahadur turned quite inactive in the final years of his life. His eyes were struck by cataract. An infection of allergy troubled him too. His backbone bent down too. He died of fever on 22 Jestha 2046 BS. He was seventy-eight years old at that time. Many an association and institute expressed condolence at his death. A memoir was published in his memory.

But the fact that in his lifetime he made incalculable contribution to Nepali literature remains uncontested. He is a lively idol of Nepali literature.

■

Khadgaman Malla: A Distinguished Writer

Khadgaman Malla is a distinguished scholar of Nepal. He is also an author, litterateur and translator. He has written several course books besides literary works, and he has translated significant works of other languages into Nepali. His contribution to Nepali literature is commendable.

Khadgaman was born on 11 Mangsir 1968 BS at Wattu-Guchcha Tole of Kathmandu. His father's name was Dibyaman Malla and his mother's name Medani Kumari. Dibyaman Malla was a government employee. So, he would be moving to different places of the country. Wherever he went, he took his son along. So, Khadgaman spent his childhood in Parsa, Morang, Sunsari, Dhankuta, and Saptari districts. When he was eleven, he came to Kathmandu and started staying with his father's sister.

He learned the alphabet from a guru at home. When he came to Kathmandu, he got himself enrolled in the fifth grade at Durbar High School. He passed the high school leaving examination from there in 1983 BS. After that, he started studying at Tri-Chandra College. Later, he completed M.A. in Hindi from Patna University of India. He is the first Nepali to accomplish M.A. in Hindi from that University.

While doing his B. A. at Tri-Chandra College, he was engaged in a job. Because of his beautiful and accurate hand-writing and at the recommendation of Rudraraj Pandey, the principal of Tri-Chandra College, he got a job at Nepali Language Publishing Committee. At that time, his monthly salary was only fifty-three rupees. After that, he became a teacher at Durbar High School. He had also worked with Fundamental Education Committee and Information Department. Later, he became the secretary of the Public Service Commission, and professor at Tribhuvan University. Once he was requested to be a visiting professor of Hindi at Peking of China. So he went there, and after returning became the secretary at the Royal Nepal Academy, and then a member of Public Service Commission. In this way, holding different posts, he worked for fifty-five years.

Khadgaman Malla also worked for different associations and institutions. He worked for Nepali Education Council, Madan Puraskar Trust, Ancient Religion Service Committee, Bhanu Secondary School Management Committee and Lekhanath Birth Anniversary Committee.

Khadgaman was profoundly interested in literature since his childhood. He used to write stories and poems. While at the college, his principal Rudraraj Pandey often inspired him to write. After he became a job-holder at the Nepali Language Publishing Committee in 1990 BS, he developed friendship with Bal Krishna Sama and Laxmi Prasad Devkota. And then, a more profound interest towards literature and writing brewed inside him. In an essay competition held at Tri-Chandra College, he bagged the first prize. His essay titled "Uddeshya" was published in the second issue of *Sharada*. This was his first published work. Later on, his essays began to be published in other magazines, too. His first book is *Nepalko Bhoogol*—the Geography of Nepal. The book was published in 1993 BS. After that, many of his books were published. He also translated a few books from English, Hindi, Japanese, and Sanskrit into English. His published books are as follows:

> **Written works:** 1. Nepalko Bhoogol, 2. Hisabko Pustak, 3. Nepal Rajya.
> **Edited works:** 1. Sajilo Nepali Sahitya, 2. Nepalko Granthasuchi, 3. Nepal Sikshya, 4. English-Nepali Dictionary.

Translated works: 1. Greece Ra Romeka Dantya-katha, 2. Andhyaroma Ujyalo, 3. Darpachurna, 4. Kasinath, 5. Baikunthako Danpatra, 6. Sarad Chandraka Kathaharoo, 7. Mahili Didi, 8. Avigyan Shakuntal, 9. Nepali Ankaganit, 10. Shinto Japanese Dharma, 11. Nepal Himalayaka Janajati.

Besides these, he also wrote several memoirs, essays, poems and collection of stories and published the same in different magazines. But these works are yet to be published as books.

Khadgaman won a gold medal for being first position holder in an essay competition held at Tri-Chandra College, a gold medal from Peking University of China, Gorkha Dakshinbahu Medal, Bal Chandra Puraskar, Bedanidhi Puraskar and *Silver Festival Coronation Medal*. He was also awarded with a Letter of Appreciation from Nepali Education Council and Letter of Felicitation from World Hindu Association. A student at Tribhuvan University has written a dissertation on the title "Autobiography of Khadgaman Malla: Personality and Works."

Khadgaman went into unconsciousness all of a sudden in the last period of his life. In the same condition, he passed away in Falgun, 2054 BS at Pashupati Aryaghat. He was eighty-seven years old at the time. After his demise, an institution named 'Khadga-Pran Memorial Cultural Trust' has been established after the name of Khadgaman and his wife Pran Maya to promote his works. The institution has done different works, including publishing and public programs. It also has published a book named *Khadgaman Malla Smritigrantha* in memory of late Khadgaman Malla.

It's a rare luck to have such a genius like him. He is a glorified personality of Nepal and the Nepalese will cherish him in their memory forever.

■

Playwright and Story Writer
Bhimnidhi Tiwari

Mechi dekhi Mahakali eutai gharko
pali
Uhi udarka santan hau hami sabai
Nepali

Khanu, sutnu yahi matra janmako
dheya ho bhane
Manushya, pashu-panchhima bhed
kele garaune?

[Extending from Mechi to Mahakali is our mother country; we all Nepalese are the children born of the same womb! If the mission of life is only to have food and sleep, what tells the difference between man, and birds and beasts?]

The above lines have been written by poet Bhimnidhi Tiwari. He is not only a poet, but also a playwright and storywriter. Apart from this, he is also known as a comedian in Nepali literature.

Tiwari was born on the last day of Falgun in 1968 BS in Dillibazaar of Kathmandu. His father's name was Lalnidhi Tiwari and mother's Nanda Kumari. His mother died when he was six. So, he was cared for and raised by his father. In order to commemorate the demise of his mother, he wrote a poem called "Dagbatti"– cremating torch.

Tiwari started composing verses even as he was a small child. His poem "Suryaghat" was printed in *Gorkhapatra* for the first time in 1991 BS. Upon getting that work published, he started publishing his creations in other magazines, too.

Tiwari loved flowers quite a lot. He was simple in behaviour. He never took addiction to anything like smoking, drinking and card playing. His fascinating desires were to herd cows, express pity upon the poor and tend a flower garden. He had opened a school during the Rana rule at his own desire. That school was closed later. He established the Nepali Literary Press in 1995 BS by importing the necessary equipments from Allahabad. He also founded the Nepali Play Association to develop Nepali dramas in 2006 BS. He himself acted in the dramas, and encouraged others to act as well.

After he became a famed litterateur of Nepal, a peculiar incident took place in his life. Despite the fact that he had cleared just grade three in accordance with the old curriculum, he finished reading all the course books of I.A., though he was caring for the education of his children. That is why he liked to appear for the exam of I.A. and filled in the form for the same. His daughter Benju and he took the examination for the degree of I.A. in the same year. The exam had been conducted at Tri-Chandra College. They both—father and daughter—were in the same room. Benju was just three benches behind him. In the exam of Nepali subject, three questions had been asked about Bhimnidhi. Benju scored twelve marks more than her father in the subject. After that, he abandoned study and completely took up writing. A piece of his famous poem goes like this:

Kaile bastachha chheuma sadakako khumchai chhati ani
Kaile herdachha purba tarpha navama lali chadyo ki bhani
Kakhi mantira jodale kara dubai chopera siu-siu garyo
Kamyo lugluga tyo gariba bichara tyasma daya garchha ko?

[A poor person sits beside the street and looks east to see if the sun in rising shortly. Breathing and shivering in cold, he is helpless;

however, nobody is there to show kindness to him.]

Tiwari served Nepali literature for life. He gave about four dozen books to Nepali literature. He also held a post in the government service. He first became the textile specialist of Domestic Enterprise Publication Office and later, a teacher at the Nepali Language Translation Council. Afterward, he became an author with Nepali Language Publication, section officer in the Ministry of Education and finally, a deputy-secretary.

Tiwari went for literary visits to many countries. He visited countries like India, Pakistan, Bangladesh, Netherlands, France, Germany, Britain, Italy, Afghanistan, Russia, and so on.

His published works include:

Plays: 1. Indradhanus, 2. Chautara Laxmi Narayan, 3. Silanyas, 4. Sahansilta Sushila, 5. Aatma-hatya, 6. Aadarsh Jeevan, 7. Ekankikali, 8. Ekanki Pallav, 9. Kashibaas, 10. Kisaan, 11. Nainika Ram, 12. Paanch Aitihasik Ekanki, 13. Putali, 14. Maharaj Bhupatindra, 15. Bibaha, 16. Nokar, 17. Matoko Maya, 18. Satya Harishchandra, 19. Siddhartha Gautam.

Poems, hymns, ghazals and muktaks: 1. Tiwarika, Aprakashit Kavita, 2. Kabitakunja, 3. Titaura and Masyaura, 4. Bayasi Bhajan, 5. Bayasi ra Bees Ghazal, 6. Varasikshya, 7. Bisphot, 8. Singha Durbar, 9. Tiwari Suktisangraha, 10. Battisputali.

Collection of Stories: 1. Samajik Kahani (from part one to ten).

Novel: 1. Insaaf.

Short Epics: 1. Yasashvi Shab, 2. Tarpan.

Collection of Essays: 1. Pandhra Pallav.

Besides these, there are many books yet to be published. Tiwari received cash prize from the government of Nepal for his plays *Matoko Maya* and *Silanyas,* and also for *Yashasvi Shav,* an elegiac epic. He received Madan Puraskar for his book of poetry *Bisphot* in 2017 BS. He was conferred other titles, including Prabal Gorkha Dakshinbahu Padak, Prakhyat Trisaktipat, Rajyaavisek Padak, Janapad Sewa Padak, and Dirgha Sewap Padak.

Tiwardi died on 19 Jestha 2030 BS in Kathmandu. After his death, many books and articles have been published. Postal Service Department has issued a postal stamp in his honor. His two daughters Benju Sharma and Manju Kanchuli are renowned in the field of Nepali literature. They have founded a literary institution named Tiwari Sahitya Samiti in their father's memorial. The institution organizes literary functions every year in memory of Tiwari.

■

Yugakavi Siddhi Charan Shrestha

Nepali hoon kathina girima
chadnalai sipaalu
Bairi nai hos tara chhu bahutai
deenamaathi dayaalu

[A Nepali I am, skilled at climbing the peaks Though a foe, I love one who's poor and meek.]

Siddhi Charan Shrestha is a great poet of Nepal. He is also called *Yugakavi*—the poet of his age.

Siddhi Charan was born on 9 Jestha 1969 BS in Okhaldunga District of Sagarmatha Zone. He studied up to eighth grade in a school there. His father Bishnu Charan Shrestha was also a litterateur. He had written a novel named *Sumati*. Siddhi Charan, however did not write any novel. He basically wrote poems. Thus, he became a poet.

In a poem titled "Barsha" written in 1997 in Newari, Siddhi Charan wrote a line 'krantibina hudaina shanti yaha'. This line, which means 'No peace will come without a revolution' irked the Rana rulers so much. Revolution, you know, is a form of change that can even change the system of adminsitration. The Ranas would never like such a change. So, Siddhi Charan was imprisoned for five years. He was the first poet to be imprisoned for writing a single word 'revolution'.

Siddhi Charan, however, continued writing and publishing. He received Tribhuvan Pragya Puraskar in 2027 BS and Prithivi Pragya Puraskar in 2045 BS for his extremely beautiful poems. Both these prizes are considered highly prestigious. Besides these, he also received plenty of prizes and letters of appreciation in his lifetime.

Leaving Okhaldunga, Siddhi Charan came to Kathmandu with his father in a small age. He has written a poem titled "Mero Pyaro Okhaldunga" in reminiscence of his birthplace. Initially, his name went into height with this very poem. Some lines of the poem are as such:

Timrai sundar hariyaalimaa
Timrai shital bakchhasthalmaa
Yo kaviko shaishav kaal bityo
Hansyo, khelyo, banakunja ghumyo
Mero pyaro Okhaldhunga.

[In the green meadows of beauteous forms
In placid laps you offered with love
This muse passed his boyhood days
Laughing, playing on the ridges green
Okhaldhunga, my beloved land!]

Among his sons, Bishwa Charan was one. But, he passed away in a small age. After the death of his son, deeply bereaved, Siddhi Charan wrote an elegiac poem "Vishwabyatha." The very poem is counted among the best poem of him.

Let's recite one of his children's poems:

Meaou meaou meaou, dudh-bhaat khaun
Chhana-chhana dhaun, musa pakri layau.
Biralo mero naun, ghar mero gaun
Aru ke bataun, ke chha khojna jaun!
Ko chha tyaha? Chyaun, chhaina kohi jaun
Chara paye khaun, meaou meaou meaou!

[Mew, I am a cat! I am fond of milk and rice
Let me go to the rooftop, catch a few of mice,
Cat is my name, listen; a home my town
What more should I say, let me look around!
Who's there, peep! There's none, so, go!
Catch a bird if you can, mew, mew, mew!]

Once Siddhi Charan wrote a poem titled "Mero Pratibimba"—Self-portrait—ridiculing himself. Actually, he had become extremely pessimistic and restless in Nepali literary society. He had written the poem to that effect. His friends and poets encouraged him. Bal Krishna Sama, the great dramatist, wrote a poem "Tero Pratibimba"—Your Portriat— in reply. Siddhi Charan gave up his cynical thoughts after the incident.

Siddhi Charan wrote 18 books altogether. Among them, six are collections of poems; nine epics; one poetic play; one more collection of children's poems; and the last one a collection of memoirs.

Following are the books he wrote:

Collection of poems: 1. Kopila, 2. Mero Pratibimba, 3. Kuhiro ra Gham, 4. Bachiraheko Aawaj, 5. Pratinidhi Kabita, 6. Yuddha ra Shanti.

Epics: 1. Urvarsi, 2. Junkiri, 3. Mangalman, 4. Aansu, 5. Vishwabyatha, 6. Sawari, 7. Jyanmara Sheil, 8. Bhimsen Thapa, 9. Aatma Bilauna.

Poetic drama: 1. Balibadh.

Children's poem: 1. Tirmir Tara.

Memoir: 1. Jailka Samjhanaharoo.

Apart from these books, Siddhi Charan has written many other things. But, these manuscripts have not been published. His mother tongue was Newari. Even in Newari language, he has written nine books on different titles.

Writing so many beautiful poems, he has become a luminary of Nepali literature. He has written many poems about the poor and the downtrodden. His poems are of practical kind. A sample is given here from his practical poem "Yugko Urdi":

Sankat pardachha manislai dhungalai ke parchha?
Asina aai phulbaarikai phulaharoo pahile jharchha.
Jasako chhaati jati bisaal, sankat tyati nai usalai
Goli lagdachha Bapuma nai kehi hudaina arulai.

[Hardship always comes to man, not upon a rock
The hail-stones hit a farm, tumble all the buds
Wider the chests people have, higher is the pain
It's Bapu the bullet hits, others all escape!]

In the above poem, 'Bapu' refers to Mahatma Gandhi of India.

Siddhi Charan edited the first newspaper *Aawaj* and the first literary magazine *Sharada* of Nepal. He became the sub-editor of *Gorkhapatra* too. He also became the chief editor of the magazine *Kabita*, published by Nepal Royal Academy.

Involving in many different institutions like Nepal Royal Academy, Standing Committee of the Royal Assembly and His Majesty Tribhuvan Memorial Committee, he worked a lot for the country.

Siddhi Charan was simple and amiable. He would help and encourage poets and authors. That's why he was dear to all.

He was soft-spoken. He listened to others and only when his turn came he talked, sensibly. His relatives and friends called him 'Kaji Dai' with love.

He passed away on 22 Jestha 2049 BS. Recognizing his contribution, the government of our country has issued a postal stamp with his name and photo. Many different associations and institutions have been established in his name.

■

Linguist Gopal Pandey 'Asim'

Suna suna bhai ho! Ma kehi
  bhanchhu
Rashwa-dirgha aadiko sawai
  kahanchhu
Bhaale naau raswa hunchha,
  pothi nanu dirgha
Jastai naati bhai raswa, tara didi
  dirgha.

[Listen children! I tell you a tale about the use of long and short vowels. The name of a male is written with a short terminal vowel; a female with long. The same is true for all males and females.]

Linguist Gopal Pandey is a prominent author of Nepal famous for such lyrical verses called Sawai, written to teach rules of grammar to children in Nepal. He has immensely contributed in the field of Nepali language and literature.

Gopal Pandey was born on 9 Jestha 1970 BS in Kathmandu. 'Asim' is his nickname. His father's name was Lila Ram Pandey and mother's name Tulka Devi. He studied at Durbar High School.

After graduating from Durbar High School, he received his I.A. degree from Tri-Chandra College. As he was involved in rescue services as a volunteer in the earthquake in 1990 BS, he failed to take the examation of I.A. that year. As a result, he abandoned formal study and got engaged in studying, writing, and publishing. He began to teach and run a literary organization. He passed his entire life in the service of Nepali language and literature.

Asim was quite inquisitive in nature from a very young age. If he encountered any event, he would ask questions like why it happened, how it happened, who caused it and how many times it occurred, etc. He would seek answers to such questions in himself. Due to this nature, he became a renowned linguist.

He loved Nepal and its people very much. In spite of scoring high marks in Nepali subject, students had to remain backward because they failed in English. So, he managed an education system to get through matriculation without having to opt English in Nepal.

Asim also thought, he should do something to pay reverence to the litterateurs of Nepal. In order to do all these things, he established an organization named Nepali Education Council in 2008 BS. He gathered prominent and novice litterateurs of Nepal and inspired them to do something for Nepali language and literature.

He worked more in the field of linguistics and grammar. His first book was a book of grammar. This book *Rachana Darpan* from part one to three, was published in 1994 BS, when Asim was just twenty-four years old. It was published by Nepali Language Publication Committee. At the age of twenty-five in 1995 BS, a book of literature by Asim was published. The name of that book was *Suniti Biraha* and that was an epic. Subsequently, he got published other books of grammar in 1997. *Raswa-Dirgha Aadiko Sawai* is one of them. He had written that book in a special metrical and poetic pattern called 'sawai.' In that book, what types of Nepali words follow raswa - the short vowels, and what types of words follow dirgha – the long vowel, have been elaborated and explained. Previously, there were no any books that could teach grammar with musicality. So, the book became very popular.

For his book *Raswa-Dirgha Aadiko Sawai*, a cash prize was given to Asim by the Department of Education and Nepali Language Publication Committee. The prize inspired him to engage himself in the field of grammar even more. And then he wrote a book named *Rachanakeshar*, a book of grammar. The book was printed in 2000 BS. From that book, students got to know many new ideas in terms of writing.

Asim thought that the book had been brought out only for adults whereas the knowledge of language and literature should be given to very young children. That's why in collaboration with a friend, he prepared a literary book named *Rashtrabhasha Sahitya* for school children. The book was included as a course book. In collaboration with a friend, he again prepared a book *Mahendra Mala* for children to read at school. The government published the very book.

These are the books he wrote:

1. Rachana Darpan (part 1, 2, 3), 2. Rashwa-Dirgha Aadiko Sawai, 3. Rachanakeshar, 4. Suniti Biraha, 5. Rashtrabhasha Sahitya (part 3, 4, 5, 6, 7, 8), 6. Mahendra Mala (part 8), 7. Samasyapurti (epic).

Besides these, he translated a book called *Swapnavasavdutta* into Nepali from Sanskrit. The play *Pramanpatra* written by him was performed in 2022 BS.

He labored hard to establish and promote Nepali Education Council. To teach students from the Council and make them take part in the S.L.C. examination, he successfully took permission from the government. In his effective leadership, statues of Bhanubhakta and Motiram Bhatta were erected. Managing time on the occasion of the birth anniversary of young poet Moti Ram Bhatta in 2013 BS, he began the programme 'Samasyapurti', a tradition of reciting poems initiated by Moti Ram himself.

In 2019 BS, collecting and editing such Samasyapurtis, he published a collection of poems named *Samasyapurti*. Some of his articles and poems had been published in different magazines. But, all these compositions have not been compiled yet as a book.

After conducting S.L.C. for twelve times from Nepal Education Council, Asim organized a convocation in 2022 BS, in which, titles and certificates were given to the students who held first and second positions in those examinations. The awards and certificates were distributed by His Majesty King Mahendra.

The polyglot and litterateur Asim organized an extensive Literary Assemblage for four days in 2010 BS from Nepal Education Council. He worked for celebrating the anniversary of devoted litterateurs for the development of Nepali language. In his effective leadership, in Ashad 2010 BS and in the same year in Bhadra, Bhanubhakta and and Motiram's birth anniversaries were celebrated at the national level with full splendor for the first time in Nepal. In 2011 BS, Kavishiromani Lekhanath Paudyal was felicitated, and the event was marked by a rathyatra—a chariot ride— to the poet. In 2016 BS, a statue of Aadhikavi Bhanubhakta— the first poet—was erected in front of Rani Pokhari. Moti Memorial Building was built in Dharan in 2033 BS in commemoration of Moti Ram, and his statue was erected there. Asim was the member-secretary of Guna Raj Smarak, Bhanu Jayanti, Moti Jayanti and Lekhanath Felicitation Committees.

Asim was awarded with Mahendra Pragya Puraskar in 2034 BS from Royal Nepal Academy. He passed away just the following year on 30 Mangsir 2035 BS. After his death, *Asim Sansmaran Grantha*—a book of reflections on Asim—was published by Nepal Education Council and an award called Gopal Pandey Asim Puraskar was established in his name.

Asim was a patriot. He had the thought that beautiful books should be written in the language of our own country, and those books should be published in many copies. Everyone should get facilities to read these books, and such books should reach all places of Nepal. As he thought so, he deeply involved himself in the service of Nepali language and literature. He is a bright star of Nepal, a true son of the country and a true devotee of Nepali language.

■

Researcher Naya Raj Panta

"PEOPLE WHO DO NOT WANT TO READ ARE PROHIBITED TO ENTER THE ROOM."

This notice hanged on the door of Naya Raj Panta. He had written this notice just under his photo at the door of his room. He actually did not let illiterate people enter his room as far as possible. He was an erudite man. He is sometimes called 'Socrates of Nepal.' He has contributed a lot in the field of Nepali literature, history, astrology, and mathematics.

Panta was born on 26 Srawan 1970 BS in Kathmandu. His father's name was Krishna Datta Panta and mother's name Yagyapriya Devi. His father died when he was just a year and half. So, he grew up at his maternal home. He learned to read from his maternal uncle. After gaining preliminary knowledge of Sanskrit at his maternal home, he began to study at Rani Pokhari Sanskrit School. After completing his study there, he went to Banaras of India for achieving higher education. He studied the principle of astrology there. He earned the degree of Acharya—a degree in Sanskrit equivalent to master's degree in the first division in 1994 BS.

He was quite shrewd, studious, and dutiful right from the time of his school days. He was interested in writing poems, and studying history and astrology. He would never go on visit, or make fun and frolic or talk unnecessarily with friends. He always went around in daura-surwal—a typical Nepali costume, a coat and a cap. He did not turn his eyes right and left while walking on the street. He always walked in deep thoughts. He never drank tea and never had snacks in hotels. He didn't like the people who did not study. To anyone he knew, he just encouraged and suggested studying. He read and wrote any time and found out new and never-thought-of things. Later, he published the creations he wrote. His first publication was "Samjhana" a poem that appeared in *Sharada* in the month of Mangsir in 1996 BS.

Panta got a job at Nepali Translation Council after returning from Banaras in Mangsir, 1997 BS. From the same year, he started teaching at Rani Pokhari Sanskrit School. He began teaching the principle of astrology at Balmiki Vidyapeeth in 2008 BS. He later became a professor at Tribhuvan University. He continually taught till 2033 BS. Thereafter, he became a member of the Royal Nepal Academy.

Panta was a spontaneous poet. One day, in 2006 BS, he was teaching mathematics to some students at his home. In the meantime, a noise of the taking-off of a plane came. The plane had just begun its flight in Kathmandu at the time. After hearing the noise, some students got up hastily and hesitantly went to look at the plane and only three remained in the room. At the moment, composing a poem in rhyme, Panta recited it to his student.

Hamra sathi aaja kaha gayechhan
Paisa papa sorna tadha pugechhan
Tystalai parkhane ho ki haina,
Yeutalai labh dota hudaina.

[Where have these friends gone? Perhaps, they have reached far away to collect money and food. Should we wait for them or continue? One cannot harvest two benefits at the same time.]

Panta ran a *gurukul*—an ancient-model school with resident gurus and disciples—and taught many students. He had made his house like a scientist's laboratory. On hearing that a man-made spacecraft and a rocket were sent to the space by America, he had tried to send rocket to other planets from Nepal on the basis of Astrology. But, he couldn't do so because of economic crisis. If that particular desire of him had been fulfilled, there would have been name and fame, prestige and dignity, and glory of Nepal in the world.

While researching on history, Panta found many mistakes written in history books. So, he opened an organization named 'History Amendment Group' to correct wrongly engraved annals. From the same organization, taking support from some other friends and his sons, he began to write factual chronicles and got them published. He began to publish a magazine named *Purnima* from the same institution since 2021 BS. He spoke and wrote only verified facts. He would die for truth. That was the reason why he is called Socrates of Nepal. Investigating facts, he wrote many books about literature, history, astrology and mathematics, and got them published.

Panta's published books are as follows:
1. Nepalko Samchhipta Itihas, 2. Itihas Sahayak, 3. Jyotish, 4. Rajpurohit Shaktiballabh Arjyalko Jaya Ratnakar Natak, 5. Aitihasik Patra Sangraha (part one and two), 6. Buddhi Binod Prasnawali ra Tesko Uttar, 7. Vidya Raksha (from part one to fifteen), 8. Gallima Phyakiyeko Kashingar, 9. Abhilekh Sangraha (from part one to twelve), 10. Sundarananda Badako Triratna Saundaryagatha, 11. Itihas Samsodhanko Praman-Prameya, 12. Shree Panch Prithivi Narayan Shahko Upadesh (from part one to five), 13. Daibagya Shiromani Laxmipati Pandeyko Ratnadeep, 14. Golbodh, 15. Maheshwacharyako Brittashatak, 16. Sumatitantra, 17. Pundit Gopal Pandey ra Unko Ghanmul Lyaune Riti 18. Prachin ra Nabin Ganitko Tulana, 19. Shree Panch Prithivi Narayan Shahko Upadeshko Sanskrit tatha Nepali Padhyamayi Vyakhya, 20. Trikonamiti, 21. Lichchhabi Sambatko Nirnaya, 22. Kalchakrako Jyotish Bhag ra Tesko Bibechana, 23. Hindu Siddhantajyotish ra Greek

Siddhantajyotishko Tulana, 24. Ratnadeep, 25. Vishranti.

Besides these, Panta has written many poems and essays in Sanskrit and Nepali languages. These compositions have been published in different magazines. They are yet to be published as a book.

Panta was honored with the titles of Gorkha Dakshinbahu Third, Shubha Rajyavisek Padak, Gyanpad Sewa Padak, and Mahendra Bidyabhusan respecting his tremendous contribution in the field of literature. He also received Aadikavi Bhanubhakta Puraskar, Tribhuvan Pragya Puraskar, Madan Puraskar, and Itihas Shiromani Baburam Acharya Sodhsamman Puraskar. Tribhuvan University conferred on him the honor of D.Litt in 2057 BS. Students of the University have conducted many researches on his personality and works.

Such a great scholar of Nepal died on 18 Kartik 2059 BS at the age of ninety. His demise left an irreparable damage to Nepal. On his death, paying tribute upon him, the King, the Prime Minister, leaders, litterateurs, literary associations and institutions, historians, mathematician, astrologists, social institution, his students, and other readers of him expressed condolence. Different magazines published special issues and features about him. A book called *Naya Raj Pant Shraddhanjali* was published in his memory.

It is said that scholars like Naya Raj are born once in a hundred years and we are unable to forget them. Making Nepali history, mathematics and astrology richer, Panta has become a man of our hearts.

■

Prudent Litterateur Yadunath Khanal

Yadunath Khanal is a prominent critic of Nepal. He was an eminent professor and diplomat. He was also a specialist in foreign affairs, and an acclaimed thinker. He has contributed tremendously for Nepal. He is a scholar whom every Nepalese should remember for ever.

Yadunath Kahanal was born on 28 Shrawan 1970 BS at Manung Village of Tanahun District. His father's name was Naranath, and mother's Tara Devi. He had learned to read and write Nepali language at the age of five. After he was six, he studied Sanskrit at his own village. He came to Kathmandu at the age of eleven, and admitted at Ranipokhari Sanskrit School. At that time, he used to read for twelve hours every day.

Yadunath cleared his intermediate exam in the first division in Sanskrit Grammar from Banaras Hindu University at the age of seventeen. He passed S. L. C. in the first division in 1992 BS, and earned his B.Sc. in 1997 BS from Calcutta University. In 1999 BS, he earned his M.A. in English literature.

Khanal was appointed professor at Tri-Chandra College in 2000 BS. In 2008 BS, he completed his Ph.D. in "Educational Thinking and Practice" from London University. He taught at Tri-Chandra College for eleven years.

Being a brilliant diplomat, Khanal got an opportunity to participate as a Nepali representative in the Afro-Asian Conference held in Indonesia in 2012 BS. In 2013 BS, he became the personal secretary to the then Prime Minister

Tanka Prasad Acharya. And then he became a secretary at the Home Ministry.

Following these services, Khanal became a member of the Planning Circle in 2014 BS. He also participated in the General Assembly of United Nations in 2016 BS and 2017 BS as the representative of Nepal. In 2018 BS, he participated the Plenary Session of the the United Nations and sometime later, the first summit of the Non-aligned Countries held in Belgrade. In 2020 BS, he was sent as the Nepali Ambassador for India, and following this, he worked as Nepali Ambassador in Pakistan, Afghanistan, Egypt, Lebanon, Sri Lanka, Malaysia and Japan. He also participated in the second summit of the Non-aligned Countries held in Colombo of Sri Lanka in 2021 BS.

Khanal worked as the personal secretary of the then Foreign Minister from from 2024 BS to 2027 BS. In the Understanding of Trade and Transportation that was signed between Nepal and India in 2028 BS, Khanal led the Nepalese side. In 2030 BS, he was appointed the Nepali Ambassador for the United States of America and in 2035 BS, he became Nepali Ambassador for the People's Republic of China, Vietnam, Cambodia, and Republic of Korea. He became a member of parliament in 2040 BS and later in 2046 BS, he became the adviser to the Prime Minister of Nepal.

Khanal also taught as a visiting professor at the Centre of Economic Development and Administration. He became the Chairperson of the Public Service Commission. He also became a member of various institutions like World-Link Council, Paropakar Sanstha, and People's Administration Federation of Nepal etc. He taught at Harvard University of America too.

Khanal was married to Kamala Devi of Syamgha of Tanahun District in 1982 BS. He has two daughters and a son. His wife died in 2047 BS.

Yadunath was keenly interested in writing since childhood. Things and thoughts that flashed in his mind would get translated into his writings. His elder brother Harinath Khanal also was a poet. So, while imitating his brother's writing, Yadunath was pulled into writing. This particular habit made him an author.

In his lifetime, Yadunath became famous as a writer. He wrote books in Nepali, Sanskrit and English languages. His first book is *Samalochanako Siddhanta*—the principle of criticism. It was published in 2003 BS. The book is considered to be the first critical book published as an original work in Nepali language. His next book of critical genre is *Sahityik Charcha*—meaning, 'literary talk'. It was published in 2034 BS. Collecting the poems he wrote in Sanskrit language, a book named *Suktisanchaya* was published in 2033 BS. *Bhaminibilas*, an anthology of Sankrit poems by Punditraj Jagannath was translated by Yadunath in the same metrical pattern as the original, and the same was published in 2055 BS. Yadunath also wrote three books in English. His published books are these:

In Nepali: 1. Samalochanako Siddhanta, 2. Sahityik Charcha (criticisms).

Translation: 1. Bhaminibilas.

In Sanskrit: 1. Suktisanchaya (a collection of poems).

In English: 1. Stray Thoughts, 2. Reflections on Nepal-India Relation, 3. Nepal's Transition from Isolationism. 4. Nepal after Democratic Restoration

Apart from these books, many of his separate articles, essays, reviews, memoirs and poems have been published. Many interviews with him have also been published. Some of his compositions and books of interview are yet to be published. All the seven books he wrote and published have been considered elegant in Nepal. If his books, which are yet to get published, are collected and launched in book forms, they could prove to be important ones.

His Majesty King Birendra gave Khanal the title 'Sardar' respecting his invaluable contribution to the country as an excellent critic, a learned professor and a successful diplomat. He also received the title Gurkha Dakshinbahu Pratham, Trisaktipatta Pratham, and Nepal Sripada Doshro Bibhusan. In 2030 BS, he was awarded the title of 'Doctor of Lodge' by Claremount Graduate School and in 2054 BS, Tribhuvan University awarded him with the title of Ph.D. He also received Bedhanidhi Puraskar and Aadikavi Bhanubhakta Puraskar—two prestigious prizes. He was felicitated by Gandaki Social Trust in 2056 BS.

Nepal's glory Yadunath died on 16 Ashwin, 2061 BS at the age of ninety-two. After his death, researches have been done on his life and work. Jayaraj Acharya has written a comprehensive book about him.

■

Accalimed Folklorist Karunakar Baidya

In the collection, publication and dissemination of Nepali folktales, the role of Karunakar Baidya has remained unsurpassed. He is also a writer known for writing books in subjects as complex as science, in a simple language, understandable to everyone.

Karunakar was born on 7 Bhadra 1971 BS at Lagankhel of Lalitpur District. Surya Man Baidya was his father and Ratna Maya Baidya his mother. His siblings were many, and the financial situation of his house was poor. The meager income from their small shop and farming was the only means of livelihood.

Karunakar learned to read and write from his own father at home. After he grew into boyhood, he enrolled himself at the Durbar High School. There he studied Nepali, Sanskrit and mathematics. Later in 1988 BS, he passed his high school from Patna University of India. After that, he came back to Nepal and admitted into the Tri-Chandra College for higher education. There he began to study physics, chemistry and mathematics. He again went to Patna to write his examinations. In 1991 BS, he passed I.Sc. in the second division. And then, he passed B.Sc. in chemistry from Patna University in 1993 BS. Following that year, he did his diploma in Ceramics. On returning to Nepal, he began serving the country with various facets of his knowledge.

Karunakar has contributed a lot for Nepal from different dimensions. He became the Manager in a ceramic factory. He began teaching chemistry as a lecturer at Tri-

Chandra College in 2006 BS. Founding the Machhindra High School at Lagankhel in 2008 BS, he taught there, too. In the same year, he contributed to open Nabin Prauda Siksyala—a school for adult education—at Tangal, Kathmandu, and taught there for sometime. In 2011 BS, he became a member of Lalitpur Municipality.

In 2014 BS, Karunakar Baidya started working with the National Education Planning Commission. But he did not stop teaching at Tri-Chandra College. He taught there for a long time.

Karunakar Baidya had a habit of expressing his feelings articulately in writing, ever since he was a small boy. So, he would instantly write down if anything touched his heart. But his first book was released only in 2013 BS. This book named *Nepal Bhasha Siksha* made him an established author.

Karunakar had a sound knowledge of three languages: Nepali, Newari and English. He wrote books in all these three language. Because he was a student of science, he wrote science textbooks, and because he was keenly interested in language and literature, he also wrote books of language and literature. Since he believed in Buddhism, he also wrote books on Buddhism. Likewise, he was interested in folk literature. He collected many folktales, edited them and published as books. He also translated some books from English language into Nepali.

There are many books to his credit in Nepali, Newari and English. All these books are not available now. Books that can be found are given below:

Science: 1. Nepalko Paramparagat Prabidhi, 2. Saral Bigyan, 3. Saral Bigyan Prashnottar, 4. Nepalka Purana Baigyanikharoo, 5. Mrittika Udhyogko Rooprekha.

Language and Literature: 6. Nepalka Kehi Boudha Kathaharoo, 7. Nepal Bhasha Siksha, 8. Nepali

Dantyakatha Sangraha, 9. Anchal Lokkatha, 10. Nepalko Lokkatha Sangraha, 11. Vishwa Prasiddha Katha (part 1 and 2), 12. Vishwa Lokkatha (part 1 and 2), 13. Ramaila Vishwakatha Sangraha, 14. Folk Tales of Nepal, 15. Nepalese Folk Stories and Legends, 16. Folklores and Legends from Pokhara.

Besides these, there are many more books Karunakar wrote. But, those books have not been published yet. There are many articles written by this author.

Karunakar was conferred 'Madan Puraskar' two times, first for his book *Mrittika Udhyogko Rooprekha* in 2014 BS and then for *Nepalko Paramparagat Prabidhi* in 2026 BS. UNESCO rewarded him for his book *Nepalko Dantyakatha* in 2038 BS. He got 'Prabal Gorkha Dakshinbahu' in 2037 BS and 'Janapad Sewapadak' and 'Dirgha Sewapadak' in 2023 BS. Nepal College Teachers' Association felicitated him on 10 Paush 2040 BS. In 2043 BS, in recognition of his contribution, an institution named 'Karunakar Sirapa' was established after his name. The institution gives awards to talented personalities of Nepal, who work in different fields.

After he became seventy-five, Karunakar fell seriously ill. He could neither eat properly, nor sit comfortably. Eventually, he passed away in 2046 BS.

The death of Karunkar Baidya caused irreparable loss in the field of Nepali folk literature. Not only in cities, but also in villages, people who read his books on folk literature are many. He is popular in Nepal because he has many best-selling books of folk literature. This is why he is immortal, even though he is no more with us in person.

■

Litterateur and Statesman
Bishweshwar Prasad Koirala

"Manis thulo banne hoina, asal bannuparchhha."

[It doesn't suffice for a man to be of high rank; he needs to have high integrity.]

Bishweshwar Prasad Koirala, the political leader cum literary writer, has delivered this message to Nepali people through his famous novel *Modiain*. He is known as B.P. Koirala, or popularly 'BP'. His brothers Matrika Prasad Koirala and Tarini Prasad Koirala are also famous for their contribution to literature.

BP was the third son of Krishna Prasad Koirala. His mother's name was Dibya Koirala. His father migrated to Biratnagar in Morang District from Dumja Village of Sindhuli District. Since Krishna Prasad Koirala fought against the Ranas, he went on exile to Benaras of India. B.P. Koirala. was born in Benaras on 24th of Bhadra 1971 B. S.

BP was named Chudamani in his naming ceremony but his father believed that he was the blessing of Lord Bishwanath and so, he was later renamed Bishweshwar Prasad Koirala. He became famous with this name.

BP underwent a lot of suffering in his childhood. He often went to school in worn-out clothes and sandals. He also sold newspapers to support his parents and to buy books. He would buy necessary things like clothes, books, and copies with his earning from vending newspapers. He attended school living on grams and water in the morning and evening. He became great and a good person by dint of diligence and patience.

There is a heart-touching incident of his childhood. BP once got an abscess on the buttocks. The wound did not heal in spite of a lot of treatment. When a doctor was consulted, he said, "An immediate surgery is a must; else it can be risky."

Surgery was costly. Chloroform, an inhaling anesthetic gas, is needed to make the patient feel no pain. His family could not afford the surgery. The doctor was even ready to operate at a lower cost; even then, his family could not arrange money to buy chloroform.

One evening, caressing the hair of BP, his grandmother said, "Dear grandson, a good man should bear troubles, and never lose his heart."

Recalling that very advice of his grandmother, BP tolerated all the pains of surgery with his jaws clenched and fists held tight, turning into another direction. He fainted due to extreme pain, but did not utter a cry. From that time onwards, he kept it in mind that a man should be extremely tolerant.

BP adored and respected his teachers at school. He was endowed with the quality to listen to others and present his own opinion cogently. He possessed all the qualities of a good student. So, his teachers were happy with him.

BP completed his B.A. and B.L. in India. While he was working as a lawyer in Darjeeling, he got in touch with Surya Bikram Gyawali. He got his first story "Chandrabadan" published in Darjeeling in 1992 with the help of Gyawali. Following this, he devoted himself to literature.

However, he could not serve literature for many years because he turned to politics. When he was imprisoned at Sundarijal Jail for eight years, he got an opportunity to study and write. He wrote a plenty of books that time.

In 2006 BS, BP's first anthology of short stories *Doshi Chasma* was published from Darjeeling.

BP was not only a litterateur but also a politician. Being influenced by Mahatma Gandhi, he participated in India's freedom movement during his school days. India was under the rule of the British. BP was imprisoned at Hajaribagh for some time for his involvement in the movement.

BP contributed immensely to bring democracy in 2007 BS in Nepal. After the revolution of 2007 BS, he was chosen the Home Minister in the cabinet of Prime Minister Mohan Samsher. He was elected in the general election of 2015 BS and became the first elected Prime Minister of Nepal. He was imprisoned when the political system changed in 2017 BS. In his life time BP passed many of his years in jail either in India or in Nepal.

After he was released from jail, BP went to India again. He returned to Nepal in 2033 BS. After his return to Nepal, many changes occurred under his leadership.

BP was worried about his nation and democracy. He wrote many books on politics and got them published. He would encourage the people he had met to get involved in politics.

During his imprisonment BP wrote many works of literature—three anthologies of stories, six novels, three autobiographies, and one anthology of poetry—altogether twelve books of BP—have been published. His works include the following:

Anthology of stories: 1. Doshi Chasma, 2. Sweta Bhairavi.

Novels: 1. Teen Ghumti, 2. Sumnima, 3. Narendra Dai, 4. Modiain, 5. Hitler ra Yahudi, 6. Babu, Ama ra Chhora.

Autobiography: 1. Afno Katha, 2. Jail Journal, 3. Atmabritanta.

Anthology of poetry: 1. Bishweshwarka Kavita.

Among his published books, *Jail Journal, Atmabritanta* and *Bishweshwarka Kavita* were published after his death.

BP suffered from cancer of throat. He went to India, Britain and America for treatment. He traveled to many countries during that time. However, he died of the same ailment later. He passed away at Chabahil in Kathmandu on Shrawan 6th 2039 BS. More than fifty thousand people took part in his funeral procession.

After his death, Nepal Government issued a ticket with his picture. Many institutions have been named after him. In addition, many roads and hospitals have also been named after BP. He has become one of the most popular persons of modern Nepal. He is honored abroad too, as a true son of Nepal. He has become the Pole Star always shining so brightly in the sky.

■

Poet Kedarman Byathit

Kedarman Byathit is a distinguished poet, a genius. He was a poet who wanted to help others and could easily identify the caliber of others. He wrote poems about events taking place daily in the society. He wrote poems that raised awareness among people. He, therefore, was a progressive poet.

His family name is Shrestha. 'Byathit' is his literary nickname. In early days, he would write his name as Kedarman Shrestha. Later he added the name 'Byathit' to it. He is known by the same literary name in Nepali literature today. The word 'Byathit' literary means 'distressed'.

Byathit's father's name was Suryaman Shrestha and his mother's name Padma Kumari. Byathit was born in Kartik, 1971 BS at Bahunepati, Bansbari of Sindhupalchowk District. That village lies on the bank of River Indrawati. He was taken to Kathmandu by his father in his early age.

Byathit would go through national and international books and newspapers at home. That is why he learned many things of the country and of foreign lands. He did not go for formal education. He just read different books and newspapers at home. He was well-acquainted with Nepali, Newari, English, and Hindi languages. Reading books in all these four languages, he obtained tremendous amount of knowledge. He also visited various places in order to know the social structure.

Among the many genres of literature, he loved poetry most and authored in the same field. Whatever the number of books he wrote all are books of poetry. He had started writing poems from his early age. But, his first collection was published only in 2003 BS. The name of the collection was *Sangam*. He was thirty-two at that time. In the same year, his another collection *Pranav* was published. An excerpt of a poem titled "Batuwaprati" by him is give here:

Pharka pharka e batuwa nani
nabadha utatira lamkera
padachinhanai pani sesha nabachne
tyo tamamaya pal pakrera
ghham-jhari bhai sukne-bhijne
ichchhako aakarshanma
kina lamkanchhau uthna saath
jeevan dhalne yo pathama.

[Return, my dear traveler;
do not move in that direction
catching hold of the dark time
where, even the footsteps do not remain.
Why do you move forward
in that direction where life is
destined to fall before a rise
driven by desires that dry so soon
like the sun now, and the rain then?]

Byathit got two collections of his poems published during the Rana rule. People who were engaged in the movement against the Rana rule tried to bring him in their favor. He joined them and revolted against the Ranas, though secretly. He would always be thinking how the Rana rule could be overthrown.

In the meantime, he got acquainted with the then revolutionary leaders. And then, he also became a revolutionary and took part in the rebellion. He supported the high-profile revolutionary leaders of that time by a large degree. Along with the four major martyrs of 1997 BS— Dasaratha Chand, Sukraraj Shastri, Dharma Bhakta Mathema, and Gangalal Shrestha—he was sentenced to eighteen year's imprisonment. His property was confiscated by the state.

On being released from prison, Byathit joined politics again. King Tribhuvan declared the end of Rana regime and inception of Democracy on 7th Falgun 2007 BS.

The poet believed that politics and literature were the two sides of the same coin. Of the two, he would not be good in one and bad in another. He believed that literature flourished because of politics and vice-versa.

After the revolution 2007, Byathit wrote many poems. He published *Nau Saalka Kabita* in 2009 BS, *Ek Din* in 2011 BS and two collections of the poems *Tribeni* and *Sanchayita* in 2015 BS.

The political situation changed dramatically after 2017 BS. Byathit endorsed the reformed system. He published two more collections of poems, *Juneli* in 2019 BS, and *Nari Rasa-Madhurya Aalok* in 2025 BS respectively. King Mahendra had appointed him the Vice-Chancellor of Nepal Royal Academy.

Slowly, the political scenario of Nepal heated up again. People began to unite against the contemporary system. Poets showed direct ramifications of the same in their poems. After this, he published two collections of the poems titled *Badalirahane Badalko Aakriti* in 2033 BS and *Mero Sapanama Hamro Desh ra Hami* in 2034 BS respectively.

Byathit also became the Education Minister for some time. He visited different places of Nepal and India. He also got opportunities to visit Russia, Britain and Germany. He had become the member of Nepali Writers' Parliament, Secretary of Nepali Literature Association, Chairman of Literature Council, and a member of Kavya Prathisthan.

During his time, he organized three to four literary conferences. The first conference was held in a boat at the confluence of the two rivers in Devghat, the holy place for pilgrimage of Hindu people in Nepal, in which the poet Mahendra Bir Bikram Shah had also taken part.

Students' movement escalated in 2036 BS. King Birendra announced a referendum. Byathit at the time was the Home Minister. He was a Congressman. Expressing his disagreement with the royal announcement of the referendum, he resigned from his post. In the same year i.e. 2036 BS, he brought out a collection of the poems titled *Meri Priyasi Prajatantrik Swatantrata*. He closely observed the violent movement of 2036 BS. Standing on the base of the movement, he wrote poems and published two collections: *Rasa Triphala* in 2038 BS and *Agni Sringar* in 2039 BS.

The poet's published books include the following:

In Nepali language: 1. Sangam, 2. Nau Salka Kabita, 3. Ek Din, 4. Pranav, 5. Sanchayita, 6. Tribeni, 7. Juneli, 8. Saptaparna, 9. Nari Rasa-Madhurya Aalok, 10. Aawaj, 11. Badalirahane Badalko Aakriti, 12. Mero Swapanama Hamro Desh ra Hami, 13. Meri Priyasi Prajatantrik Swatantrata, 14. Rasa Triphala, 15.Agni Sringar, 16. Dristi Satya Shristi Sundar, 17. Mero Darpan Chaar Dashakko Nepal, 18. Arko Euta Kurukshetra.

In Hindi language: 1. Hamara Desh Hamara Swapna, 2. Trayi, 3. Agni Shringar, 4. Tewar Kabita ka Sandarbha Aaj ka.

In Newari language: 1. Pratiksha, 2. Diwas Chitra, 3. Khawabipya: Gu Me, 4. Chhwas.

In English language: 1. Selected Poems (In this collection, his poems translated into English have been included.)

Critics say that his poems often deal with themes of nature and humanity, love, kindness and irony. He was awarded with Prithivi Pragya Puraskar, Jagadamba Puraskar, Sita Ram Puraskar, and Bedhanidhi Puraskar for his wonderful poems.

Let us look at his poem titled "Mero Udan Chandralokma" to have a glimpse of the type of poetry he wrote.

Hunchha malai yaha
Kahile kahi nirasha
Artha nikaloon kasari
Bujhi nasaknu bhasha
Aagoma boso paglejhai
Kanch phutejhai swar matra
na pad, na vakya
kewal dhawni matra.

[Often, here
I am besieged by intense hopelessness.
How am I to interpret this?
It's a language, not understandable.
Like fat melting in flames
like glass, breaking into fragments
all I hear is a sound
neither a verse, not any sentence
but sound; mere sound.]

Byathit, in his lifetime, established a prize trust named Byathit Kavya Puraskar Kosh with an objective to give prizes to poets through an organization called 'Sahityik Patrakar Sangh' in his own village. Even today, the prize is distributed to poets who contributed in the genre of poetry considerably.

Byathit was a complete poet. He was keenly fond of reciting and talking about poems by inviting critics at home. He died on 25 Bhadra 2056 BS at his own home at Jyatha of Kathmandu. He was suffering from asthma and diabetes.

In this old age, though he had grown quite weak, he would often be seen walking here and there. Only a couple of days before he died, he became bed-ridden.

At the death of Byathit, Nepal lost a charismatic poet. A poet like him rarely gets born.